TOP SELECTION:

The Finest International Political Cartoons of our Time

edited by *Joe Szabo*

WITTYWORLD BOOKS, *a division of WittyWorld Publications*

Book Design:
Joseph Starlight

Cover Illustrations:
Valeriu Curtu (upper left)
Mike Peters (lower left)
António Moreira Antunes (right)

Back cover:
Jules Feiffer

The editor would like to extend special thanks to
John A. Lent
for his expert assistance.

ISBN: 0-9631600-1-X

WittyWorld Publications
P.O. Box 1458, North Wales, PA 19454
United States of America

Contents

Reflections 1
The Gulf War 5
Hussein 23
Kurdistan 28
Arab Oil 30
Hostages 31
Eastern Europe 32
Poland 36
Cuba 38
Haiti 40
Canada 41
England 42
Germany 43
South Africa 46
El Salvador 48
India 49
China 50
The End of an Era 52
Russian Economy 80
Dangers 92
Third World 94
US Helping Hand 102
Censorship 104
AIDS 106
Economy 108
Car Wars 112
NATO 116
War 117
Yugoslavia 122
Middle-East 128
Arab-Israeli Peace Talks 137
New World Order 156
European Unification 160
Index 165

TOP SELECTION:

The Finest International Political Cartoons of our Time

edited by Joe Szabo

Reflections

Generally cautious about using superlatives, I was hesitant about the title of this book. But as I repeatedly browsed through the material, I became comfortable that "finest" is not an overstatement. The cartoons here are indeed a true reflection of the very best political cartoons spanning the world today.

This collection was intended to be much more than just a useful tool for political science and social studies classes. The primary goal was to gather the most imaginative and best drawn cartoons from around the world, and give them a deserving presentation.

The styles, formats, and sometimes even the purposes of political cartoons differ greatly from country to country. Although there are exceptions, in Eastern Europe, Latin America and Third World countries, political cartoons are rarely explicit, pin-pointing particular persons, parties or governments. Perhaps because they have operated under dictatorial rule for decades, many of these cartoonists play it safe, tackling general and, thus, less career-threatening issues, such as the environment, poverty, war, censorship or the economy.

Most of these cartoons, silent and symbolic, fall under a visual commentary category, the type that most United States newspapers use for op-ed illustrations. Few countries have the tradition of providing space for editorial/political cartoons in newspapers that exists in the United States, England or France, and few international cartoonists have the luxury of a full time staff position on a major daily. Those who do, however, are probably the best read and recognized authors anywhere in the world.

These multiple talented visual journalists can be merciless enemies of the unjust, the corrupt and the ineffective public servant. From Boss Tweed to President Nixon, politicians know how painfully effective cartoonists can be. "Dictators of the right and the left fear the political cartoonist more than they do the atomic bomb" said satirical columnist Art Buchwald. Some of them have been driven from office as cartoonists greatly contributed to public awareness of their shady activities. Others tried to patronize or otherwise silence pesky cartoonists with bribery, intimidation, censorship or worse.

Cartoonists have been imprisoned for doing their jobs in Southeast Asia, Eastern Europe, Latin America and Africa. In 1987, the murder of a Palestinian cartoonist gave chilling proof to Buchwald's statement. Naji Salim al-Ali was shot in London after having received more than one hundred death threats. Fortunately, however, most cartoonists in democracies are able to do their jobs without harassment.

In this book, I have attempted to pull together the wittiest, most original, and most skillfully drawn cartoons of differing political hues done in the recent past. The selected works were culled from a search of cartoons from 48 countries.

American cartoonists **Auth**, **Conrad**, **Feiffer**, **MacNelly**, and **Oliphant** hardly need to be introduced. They have consistently produced meaningful and visually exciting cartoons for decades. Including them, eleven Pulitzer Prize winners are exhibited in this book; some (**MacNelly**, **Conrad**, and **Szép**) won more than once.

The international cartoonists too, are highly acclaimed and renowned. There are legends here, including the Russian **Zlatkovsky**, **Peterson** from Canada, Sweden's **EWK**, **Bas** from Athens, the Turkish **Turhan Selçuk**, and the Hungarian-born Israeli **Ze'ev**. There is a younger generation of stars as well, such as the Parisian **Plantu**, the Portuguese **António**, the British **Griffin**, **Kemchs** from Mexico City, **Deng Coy Miel** from the Philippines, **Botezatu** from Romania, **de Angelis** from Italy, and the Croatian **Felix**. Singling out a few is not meant to slight others; by their status in cartooning, all of the artists represented in this book deserve a special mention.

The strength of some of these cartoonists is their unusual perception and wit, while others are blessed with phenomenal artistic skill. Some are at their best when ridiculing the ridiculous; many are serious and painfully hard-hitting, and others utterly funny.

The representation is diverse, allowing readers to see the best samples available from countries (such as China, Croatia, Ecuador, Iran, Peru or Singapore) not usually accessible to Western culture, and vice-versa.

Last year was particularly rich in events of international concern. It is interesting to see the distinct, yet somewhat homogeneous perceptions of worldwide cartoonists on topics like the Gulf war, the complete disintegration of a superpower, and the Arab-Israeli peace negotiations.

The perceptions and approaches may be different, but there is hardly any disagreement concerning basic human rights and common sense. These cartoonists' weapon may be poisonous, but their intentions are definitely just, pure, and noble. And they are always on our side.

During the Gulf War the military's control over the press drew criticism from **Collignon** and **Conrad**. **Auth**, **Danziger** and **Yaoning Zhang** were horrified over the tremendous damage Iraq's dictator did to nature. **Henninger**, **Gerd**, and **Tomaschoff** felt for the disadvantaged immigrants and former East Germans. **Peterson**, **Botezatu**, **Janssen**, **Borgman**, **Kal** and **Conrad** had sharp and original reactions to the rapid disintegration of the once powerful communist machine and its slow metamorphosis. **Auth**, **Rodewalt**, and **Keefe**'s irony and **Zlatkovsky**'s powerful symbolism about the Russian economic reality also highlight this collection.

The silently screaming cartoons of **Vlahovic** and **Al-Awadi**, drawing attention to Third World agonies, are extraordinary examples of the cartoonists' creative talent coupled with super sensitivity.

I could go on and on. Remarkable creativity and proficiency with tremendous visual communication skills everywhere.

Tackling the AIDS issue, **Signe Wilkinson**, the first female cartoonist ever to win the Pulitzer Prize (1992), demonstrates her unusual ability to mix the hard-hitting with feminine subtlety. **Plantu**'s implication that Serbia's unnecessary destruction of the uniquely intact medieval town of Dubrovnik was worst than barbaric, is another example of political cartoonists advocating common sense and guarding humanitarian values.

Sampling further, it's impossible not to burst into laughter at **Mike Peters**' cartoon about the Arab-Israeli peace talks. The 1992 winner of the Reuben Award is consistently funny, a rarity in a profession of angry soldiers of the drawing pen.

But it does not matter who did what. It's why and how it was done. That is why we ought to bow before these 124 unusual pen-handlers, who elevated us to the heights of their philosophical sophistication and extraordinary artistic talent.

ANTÓNIO MOREIRA ANTUNES
Portugal

JULES FEIFFER
USA

PETAR PISMESTROVIC
Austria

JOS COLLIGNON
Netherlands

PANCHO
(FRANCISCO GRAELLS)
France

MARK LYNCH
Australia

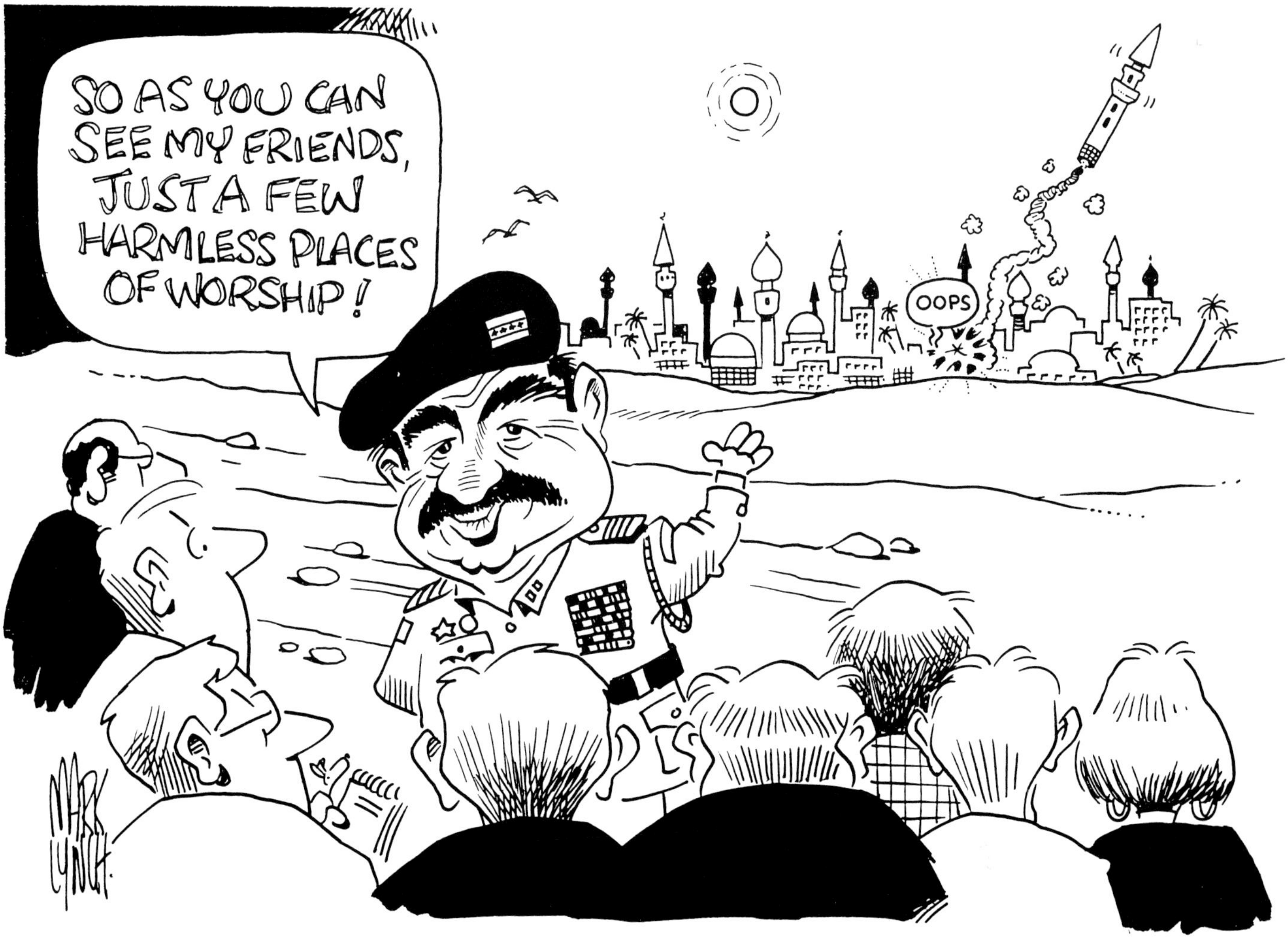

SO AS YOU CAN SEE MY FRIENDS, JUST A FEW HARMLESS PLACES OF WORSHIP!

OOPS

MARK LYNCH

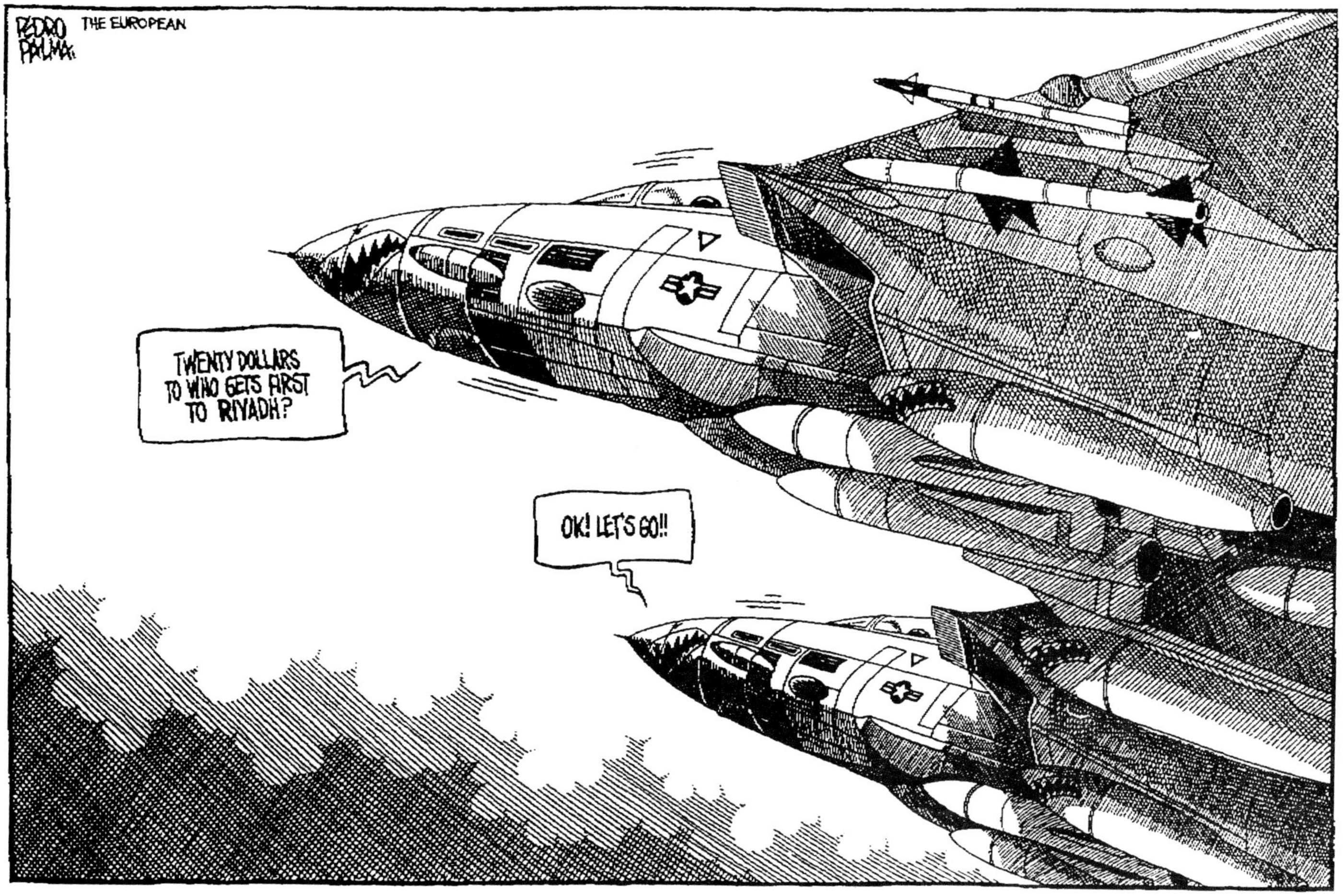

PEDRO PALMA THE EUROPEAN

TWENTY DOLLARS TO WHO GETS FIRST TO RIYADH?

OK! LET'S GO!!

PEDRO PALMA
Portugal

CHARLES GRIFFIN
England

TONY AUTH
USA

ALADIN SAAD
Egypt

AUTH
OFFICE OF THE PRESIDENT
CNN
KUWAIT
CAN'T A MAN EAT IN PEACE?
ERSAL PRESS SYND.

PAUL CONRAD
USA

G. A. LATIFI
Iran

SHMULIK
(SHEMUEL A. KATZ)
Israel

JIM BORGMAN
USA

PAT OLIPHANT
USA

'THIRTY THOUSAND FOR DINNER LAST NIGHT, FIFTY THOUSAND FOR BREAKFAST TODAY, EIGHTY THOUSAND FOR LUNCH—IT'S TIME TO CALL OFF THE DAMN WAR!'

"I PRAY THAT GOD WON'T FORCE ME TO USE UNCONVENTIONAL WEAPONS."
—SADDAM HUSSEIN

PAUL CONRAD
USA

PAT OLIPHANT
USA

GOOT– YOU OWE
US THIRTEEN
BILLION DOLLARS
BILL
OLIPHANT

TONY AUTH
USA

JEFF DANZIGER
USA

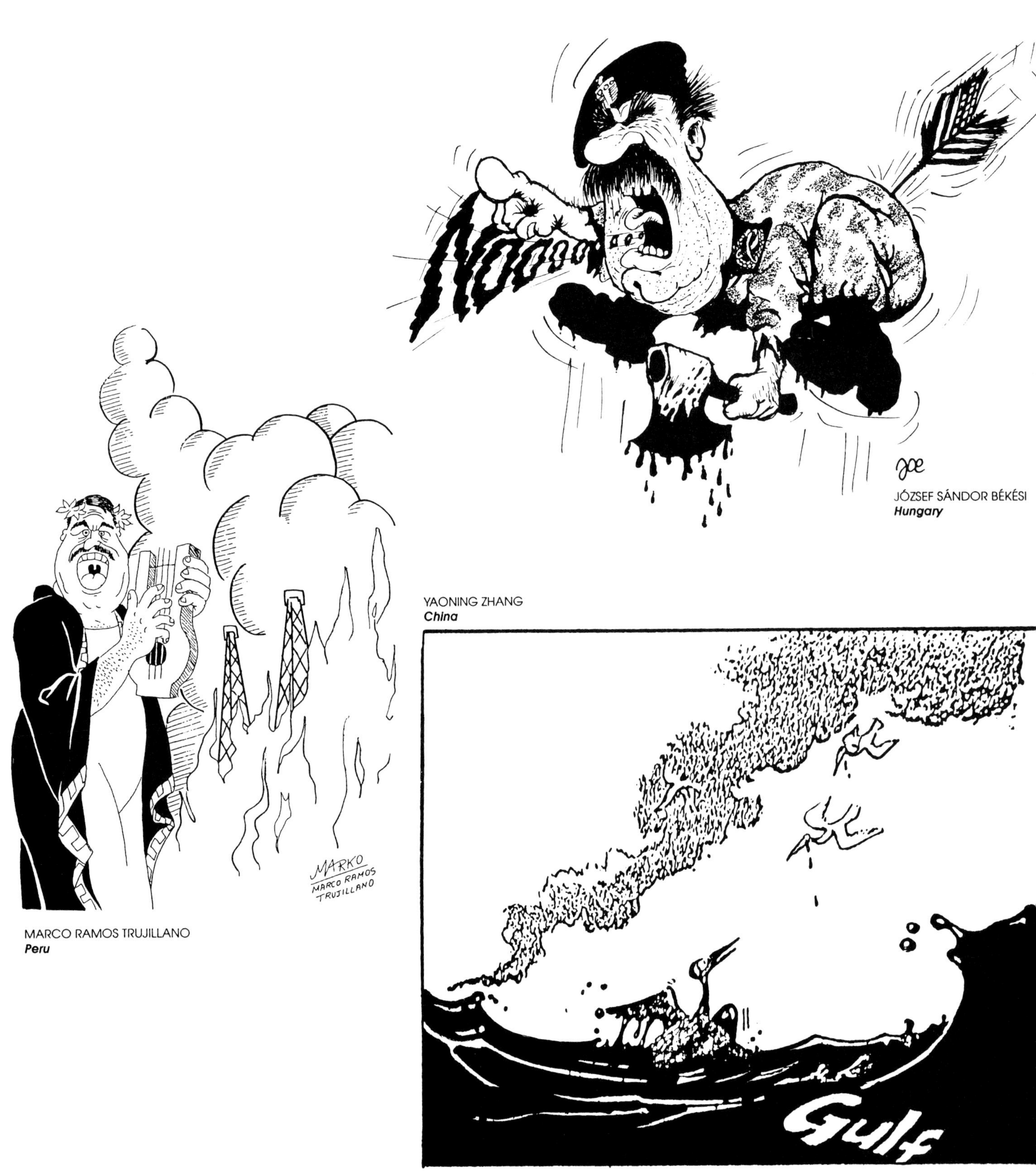

JÓZSEF SÁNDOR BÉKÉSI
Hungary

MARCO RAMOS TRUJILLANO
Peru

YAONING ZHANG
China

"Mother, is this the Dead Sea?"
"No, this is the New Dead Sea."

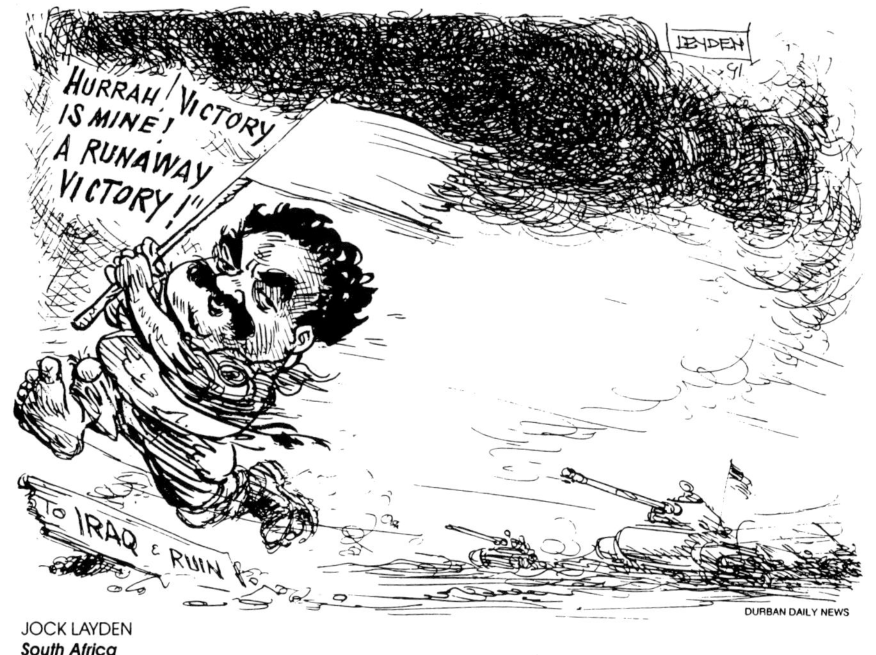

"HURRAH! VICTORY IS MINE! A RUNAWAY VICTORY!"
TO IRAQ & RUIN
LAYDEN
DURBAN DAILY NEWS

JOCK LAYDEN
South Africa

TONY GROGAN
South Africa

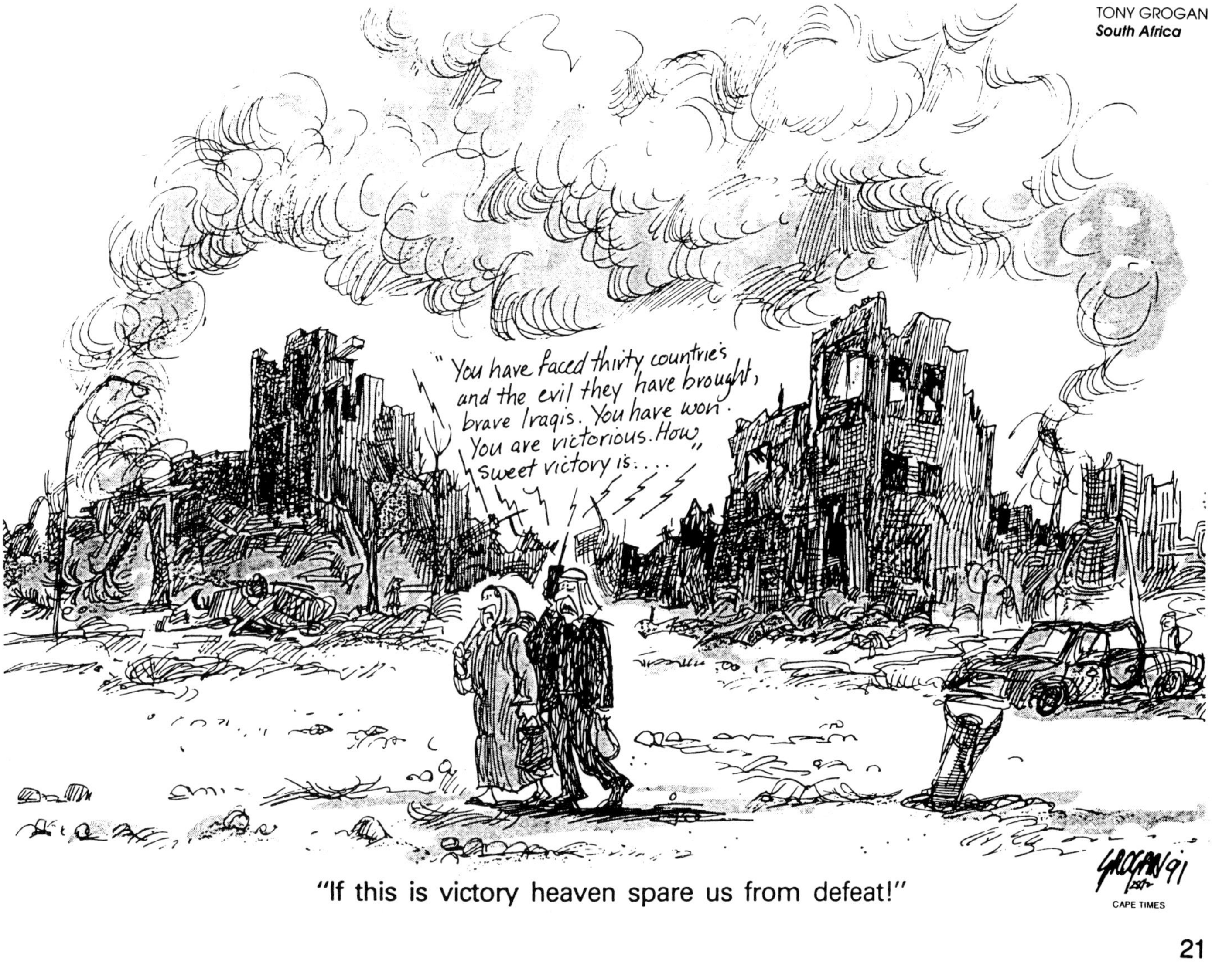
"You have faced thirty countries and the evil they have brought, brave Iraqis. You have won. You are victorious. How sweet victory is...."
GROGAN '91
CAPE TIMES

"If this is victory heaven spare us from defeat!"

DANA SUMMERS
USA

FRANCISCO CAJAS
Equador

Cajas

CARTOONISTS & WRITERS SYNDICATE

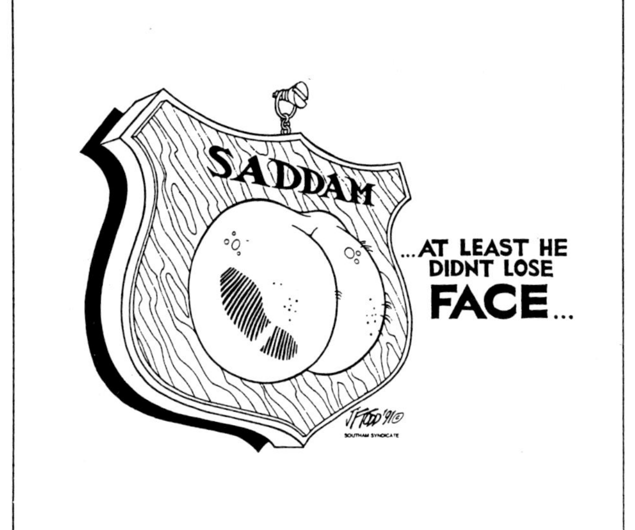

JAMES TODD
Canada

DAVID SEAVEY
USA

Bortolotti

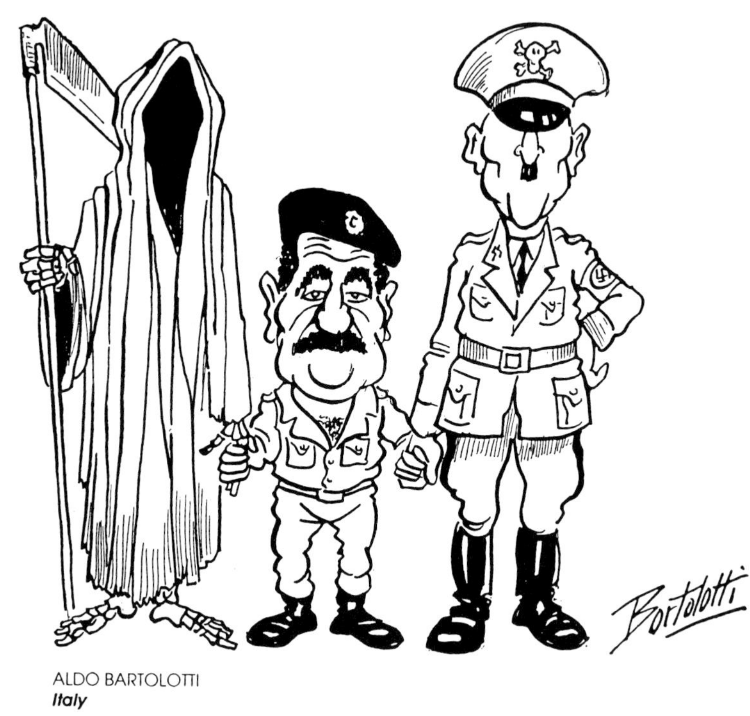

ALDO BARTOLOTTI
Italy

HORST HAITZINGER
Germany

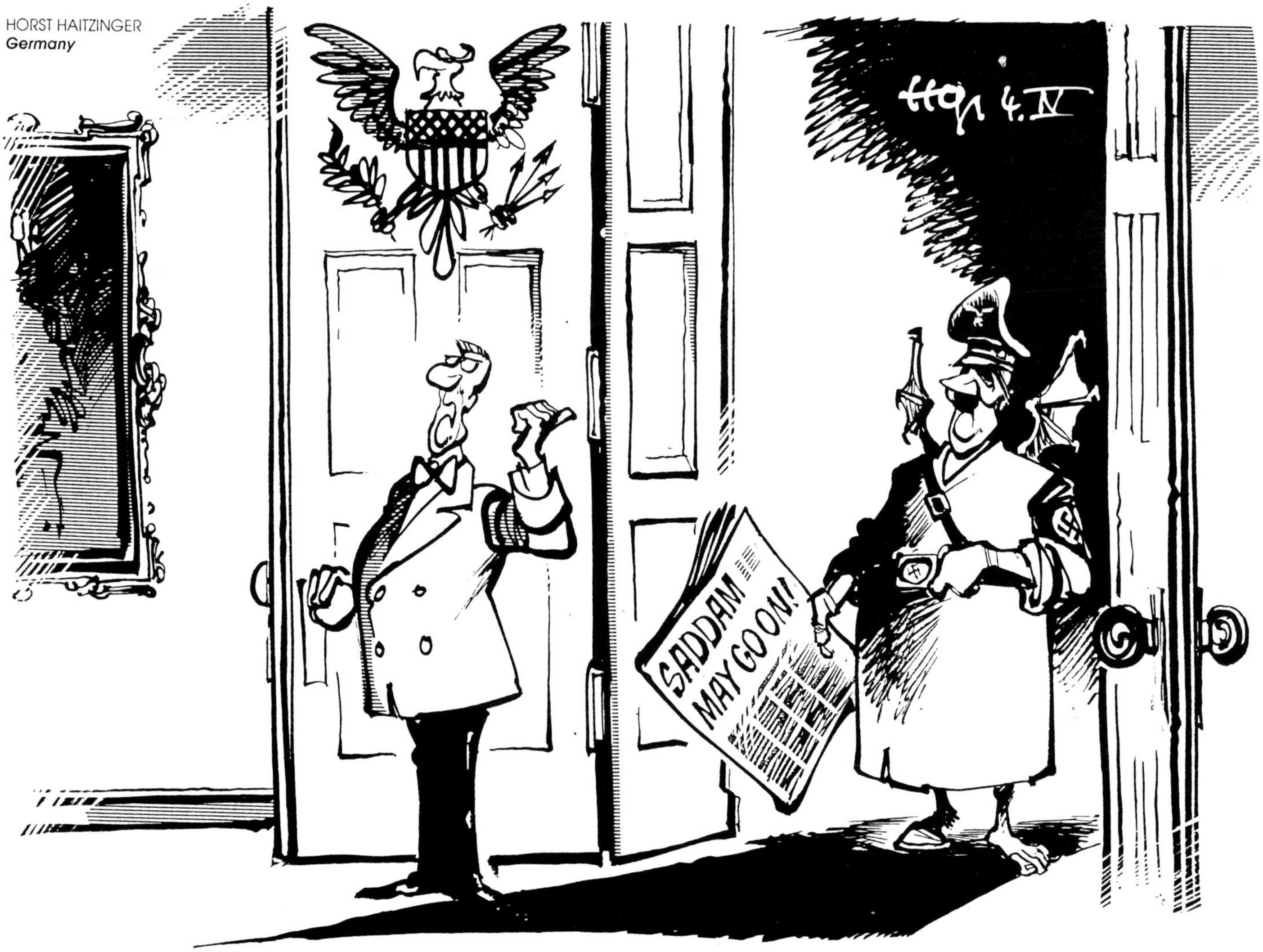
SADDAM MAY GO ON!

Mr. President, here is someone who feels discriminated against!...

JAVAD ALIZADEH
Iran

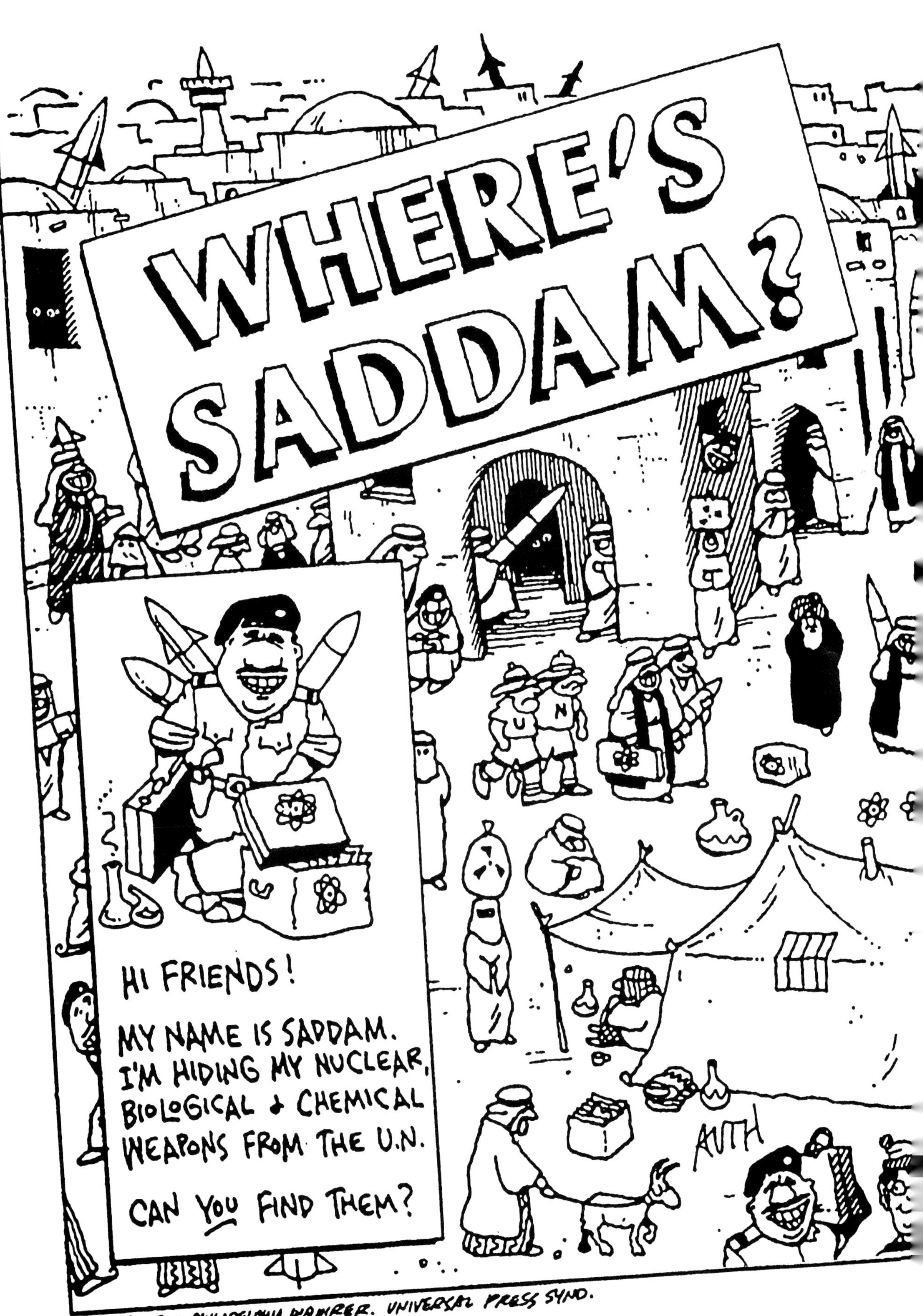

TONY AUTH
USA

ROAR HAGEN
Norway

JOSH BEUTEL
Canada

PAUL SZÉP
USA

DESERT STORM VICTO

SZEP
THE BOSTON GLOBE

" DAMN! . . . . . IT'S RAINING KURDS ON MY CHARADE!! "

Oil junkie

JEFF MACNELLY
USA

MARTYN TURNER
Ireland

VLADIMIR BALCAR
Czechoslovakia

ED STEIN
USA

JIM BORGMAN
USA

NEWS

JIMBORGMAN

"EASTERN EUROPE SUBDIVIDED AGAIN TODAY...."

FIKO FIKOV
Bulgaria

PAT OLIPHANT
USA

GUSTAVE EWERT KARLSSON
Sweden

SZYMON KOBYLINSKI
Poland

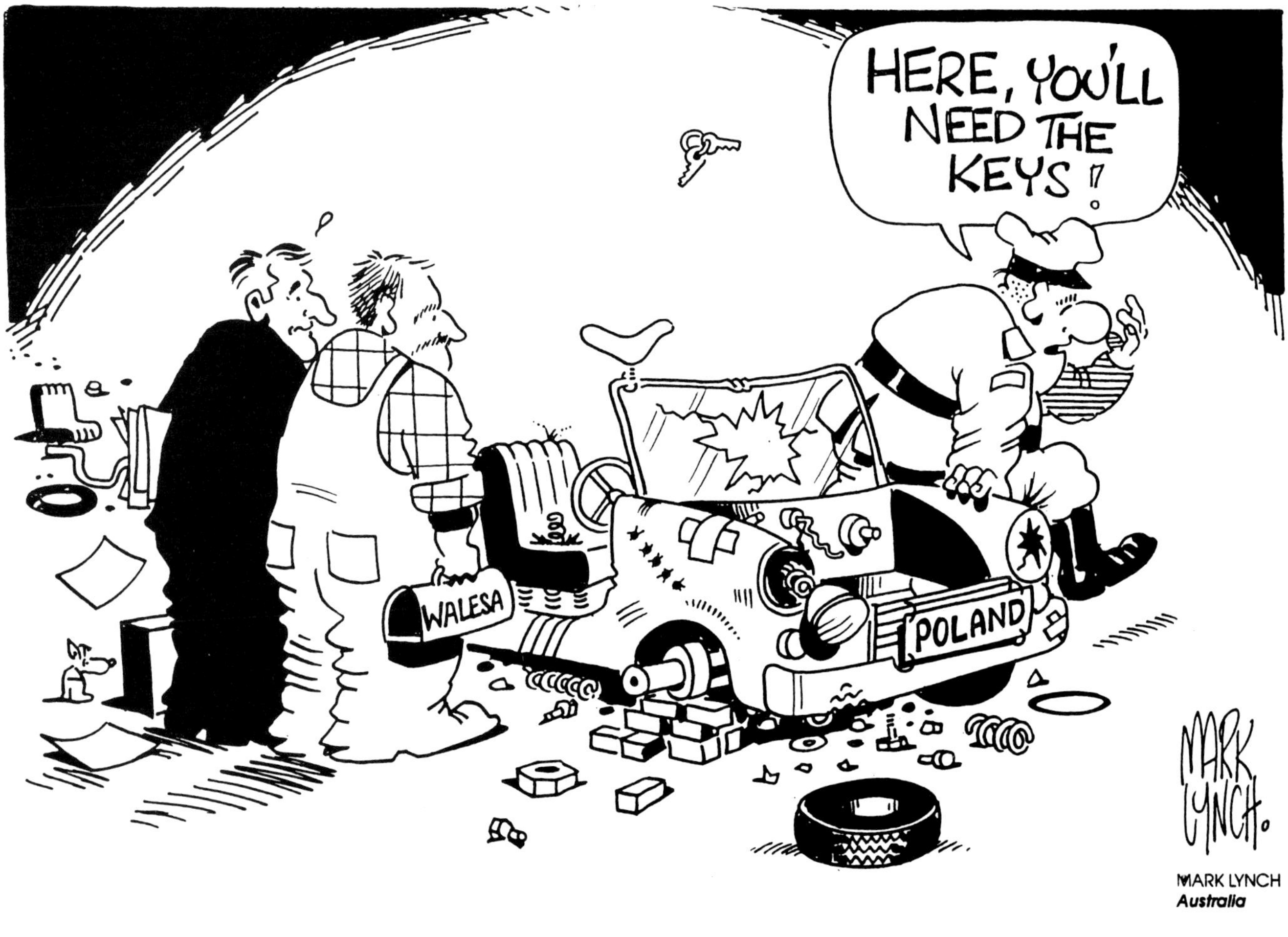

HERE, YOU'LL NEED THE KEYS!

WALESA

POLAND

MARK LYNCH

MARK LYNCH
Australia

ANTONI CHODOROWSKI
Poland

MACNELLY Chicago Tribune
FREEDOM

GUJJAR
(B. G. GUJJARAPPA)
India

JEFF MACNELLY
USA

DOUG MARLETTE
USA

QUEBEC
CANADA
RODEWALT CALGARY HERALD 2/22 '91

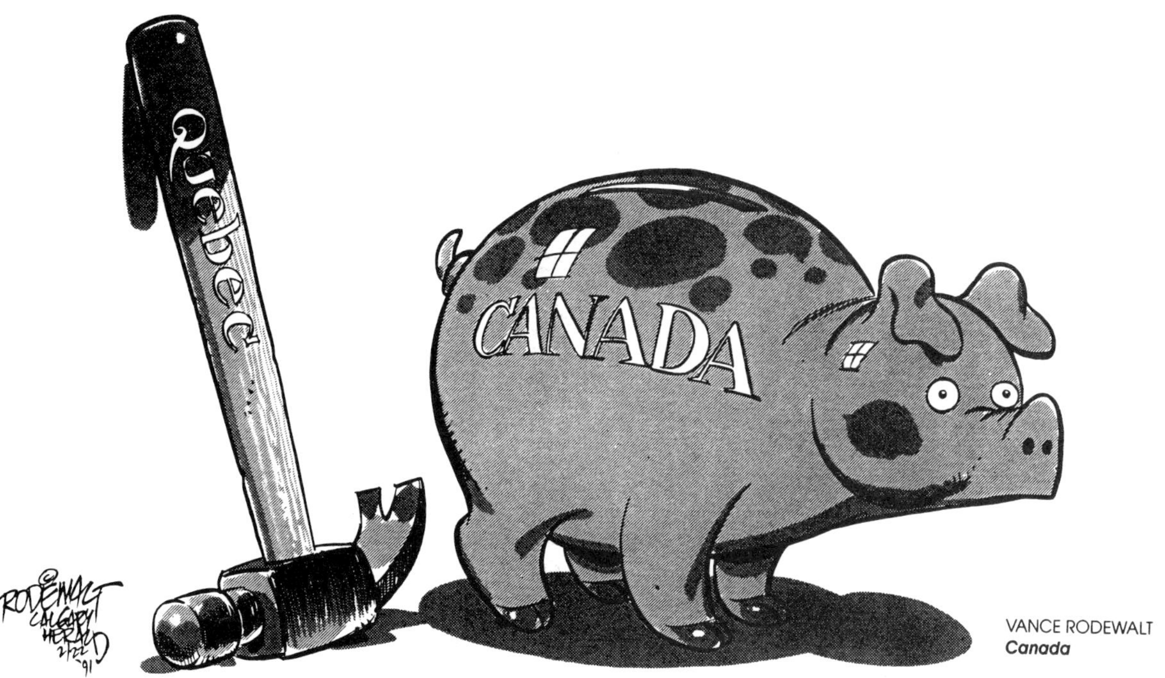

VANCE RODEWALT
Canada

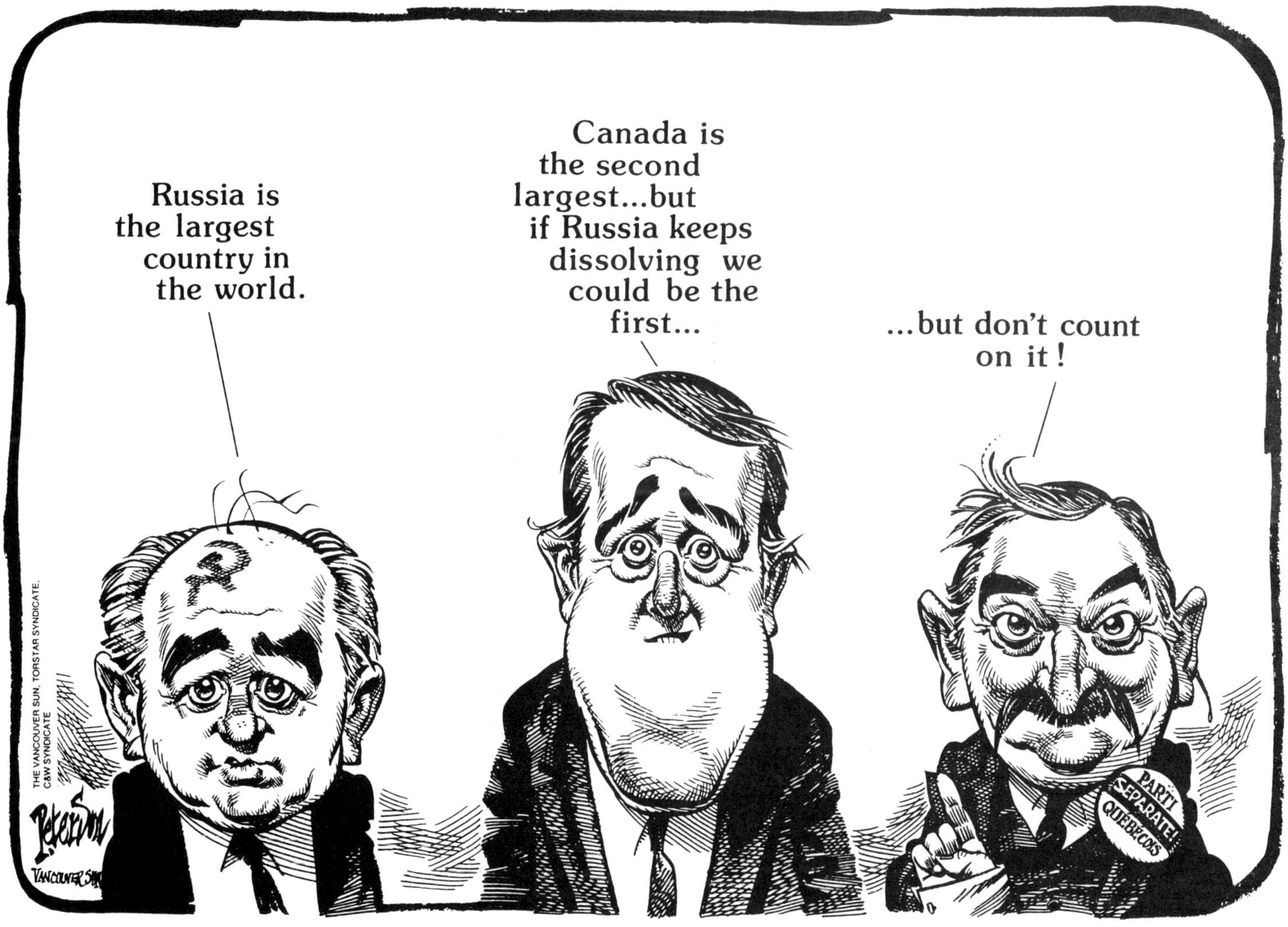
Russia is the largest country in the world.
Canada is the second largest...but if Russia keeps dissolving we could be the first...
...but don't count on it !
PARTI SEPARATE! QUEBECOIS
THE VANCOUVER SUN, TORSTAR SYNDICATE, C&W SYNDICATE
PETERSON VANCOUVER SUN

ROY PETERSON
Canada

CHARLES GRIFFIN
England

"You there! Get that lens-cap <u>on</u>!"

CHARLES GRIFFIN
England

UNLEADED NORTH SEA PETROL

POLICE

BUY BRITISH

POLICE

Griffin

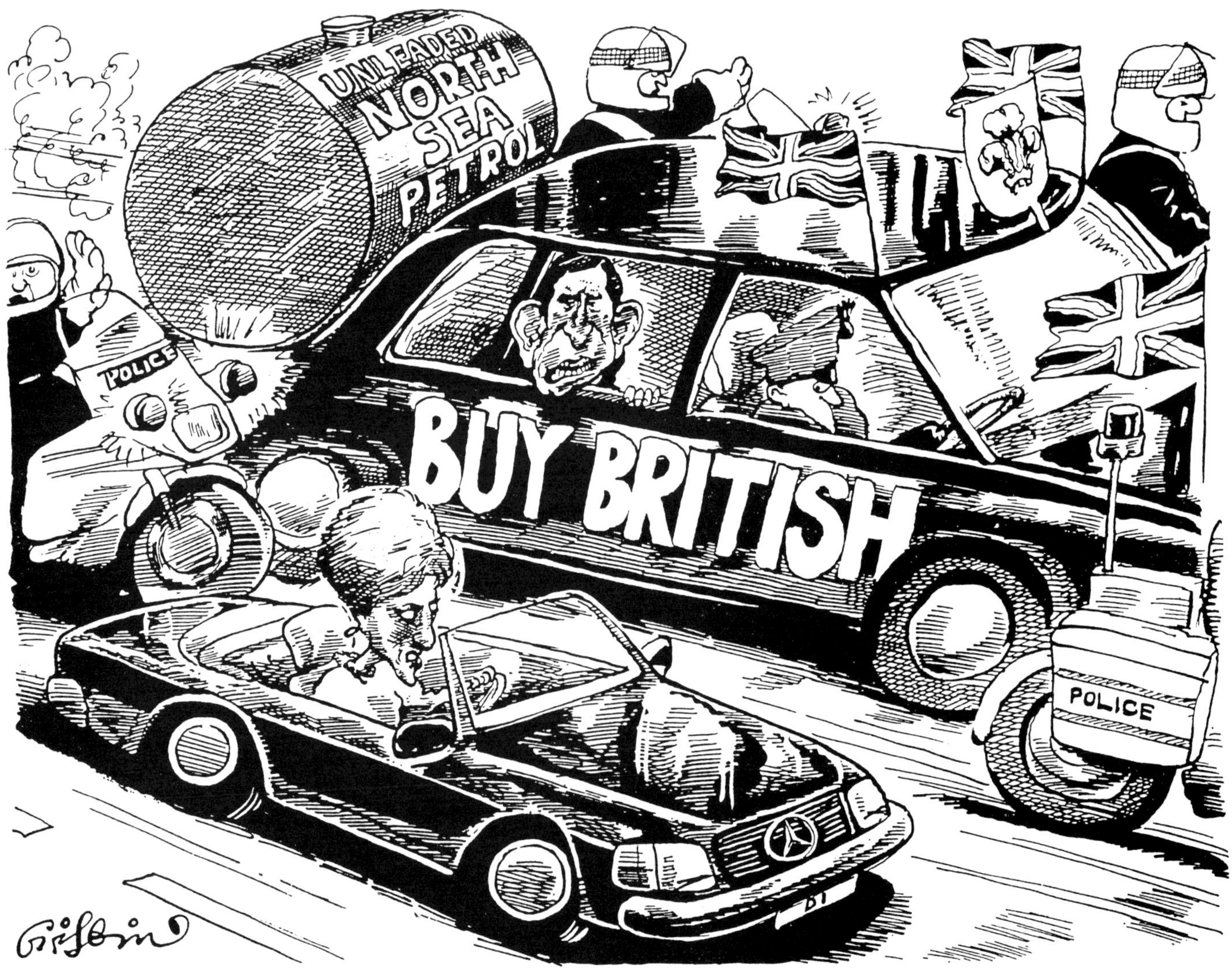

"Have you no conscience, woman?"

BARBARA HENNIGER
Germany

German honeymoon

The new
German wall

KARL GERD
Germany

JAN TOMASCHOFF
Germany

RAINER HACHFELD
Germany

KEVIN KALLAUGHER
USA

BALTIMORE SUN - C&W SYNDICATE

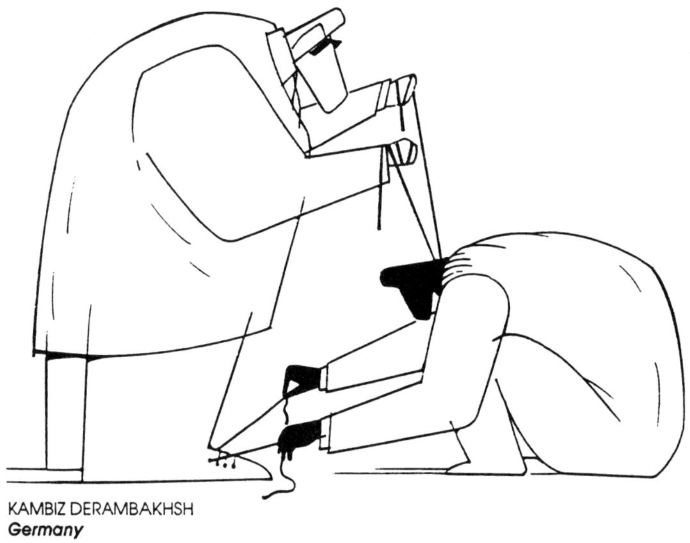

KAMBIZ DERAMBAKHSH
Germany

DAVID ANDERSON
Canada

DANZIGER

THE CHRISTIAN SCIENCE MONITOR
LOS ANGELES TIMES SYNDICATE.

JEFF DANZIGER
USA

PREBEN OLESEN
Denmark

NAPOLEON HAM
Honduras

Mike Keefe '91 THE DENVER POST

MIKE KEEFE
USA

INDIA'S GOD OF POLITICS

PRABHAKAR
WAIRKAR
India

DOMINIQUE JACQUEMIN
Belgium

SERDU
(SERGE DUHAYON)
Belgium

DANA SUMMERS
USA

WASHINGTON POST WRITERS GROUP

PLEASE
TAKE A
NUMBER
THANK YOU
1956
1848
1924
THE VANCOUVER SUN, TORSTAR SYNDICATE, C&W SYNDICATE

ROY PETERSON
Canada

THE END OF AN ERA

MARCO DE ANGELIS
Italy

CARTOONISTS & WRITERS SYNDICATE

FRITZ BEHRENDT
Netherlands

MARXISM

CASTRO

LENINISM

KIM IL SUNG

CARTOONISTS & WRITERS SYNDICATE

F. Behrendt

ROBERTO FONTANARROSA
Argentina

PAVEL BOTEZATU
Romania

BAS. MITROPOULOS
Greece

WORKERS OF THE WORLD UNTIE!

Somehow it lost something in the translation over the years...

PETERSON
VANCOUVER SUN

THE VANCOUVER SUN, TORSTAR SYNDICATE, C&W SYNDICATE

ROY PETERSON
Canada

THE END OF AN ERA

ALPER SUSUZLU
Turkey

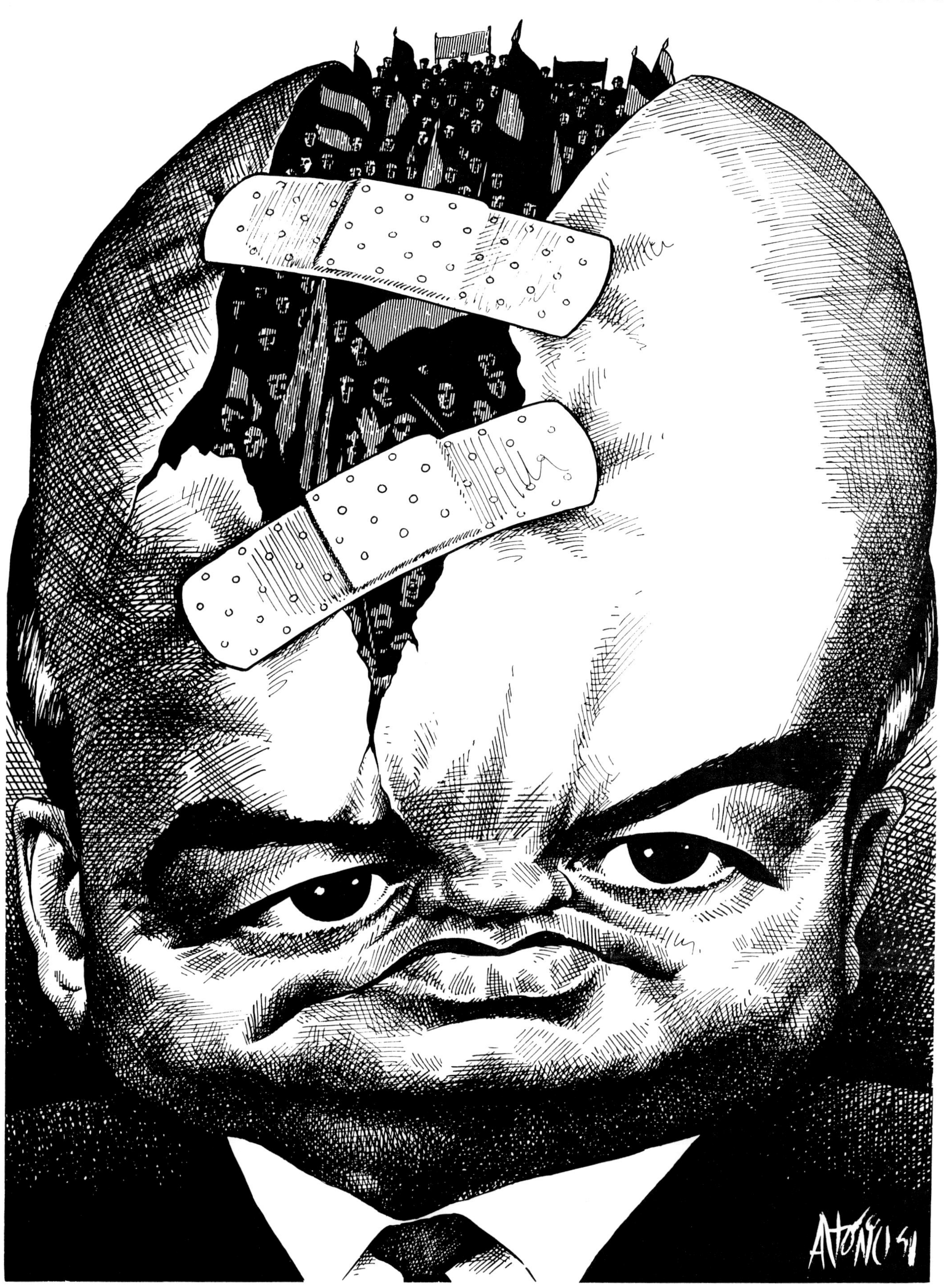

ANTÓNIO MOREIRA ANTUNES
Portugal

VLADIMIR BALCAR
Czechoslovakia

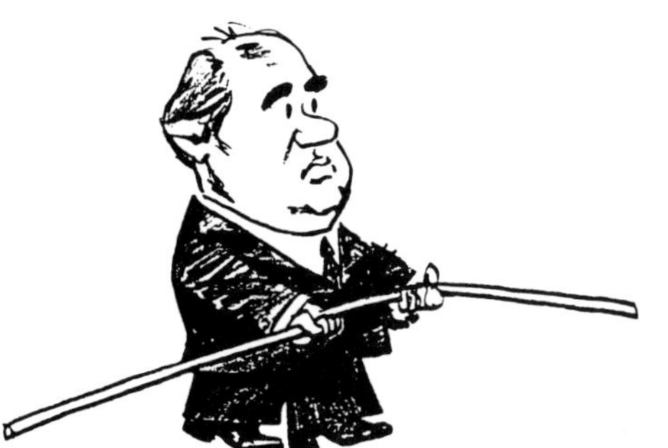

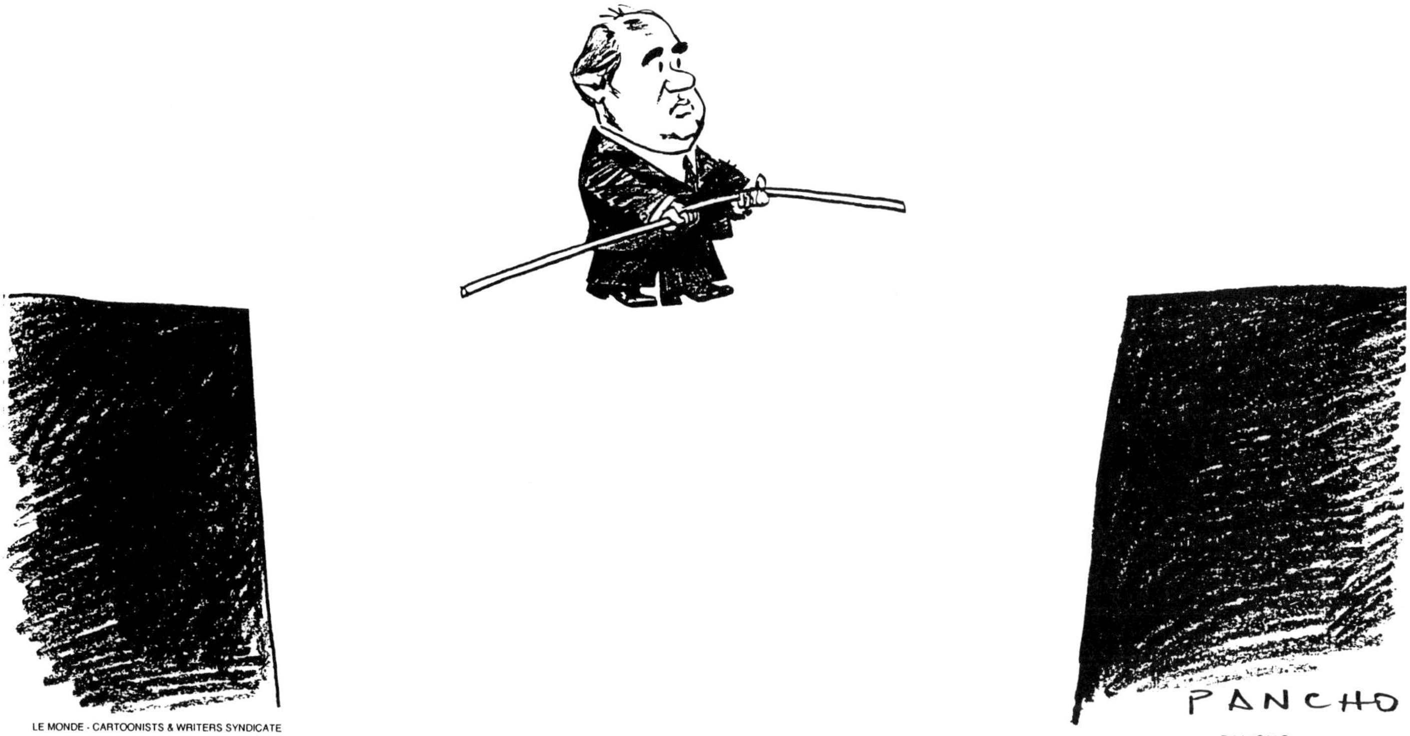
PANCHO
LE MONDE - CARTOONISTS & WRITERS SYNDICATE

PANCHO
(FRANCISCO GRAELLS)
France

PAT OLIPHANT
USA

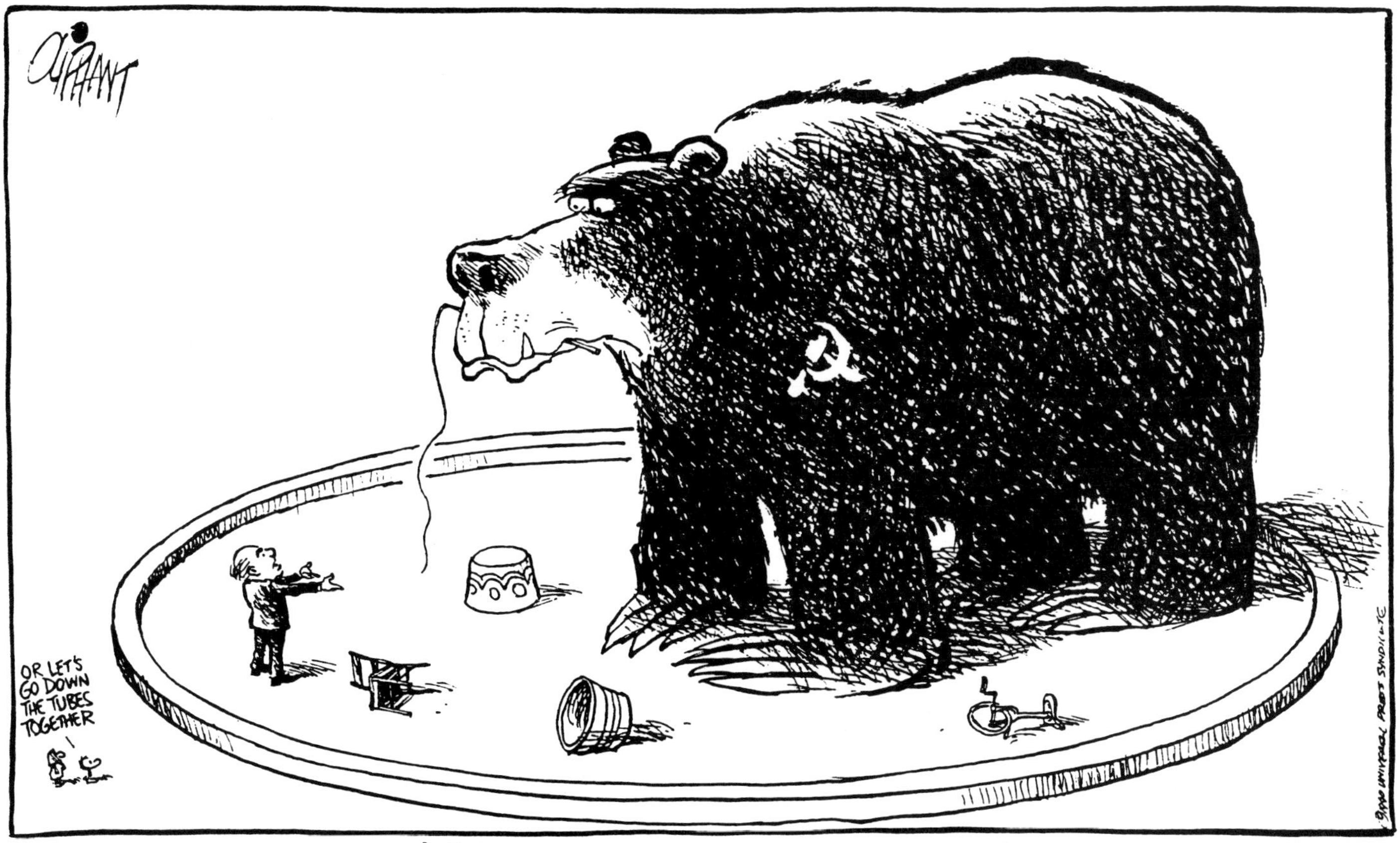
OLIPHANT
OR LET'S GO DOWN THE TUBES TOGETHER

'COME, LET US REASON TOGETHER.'

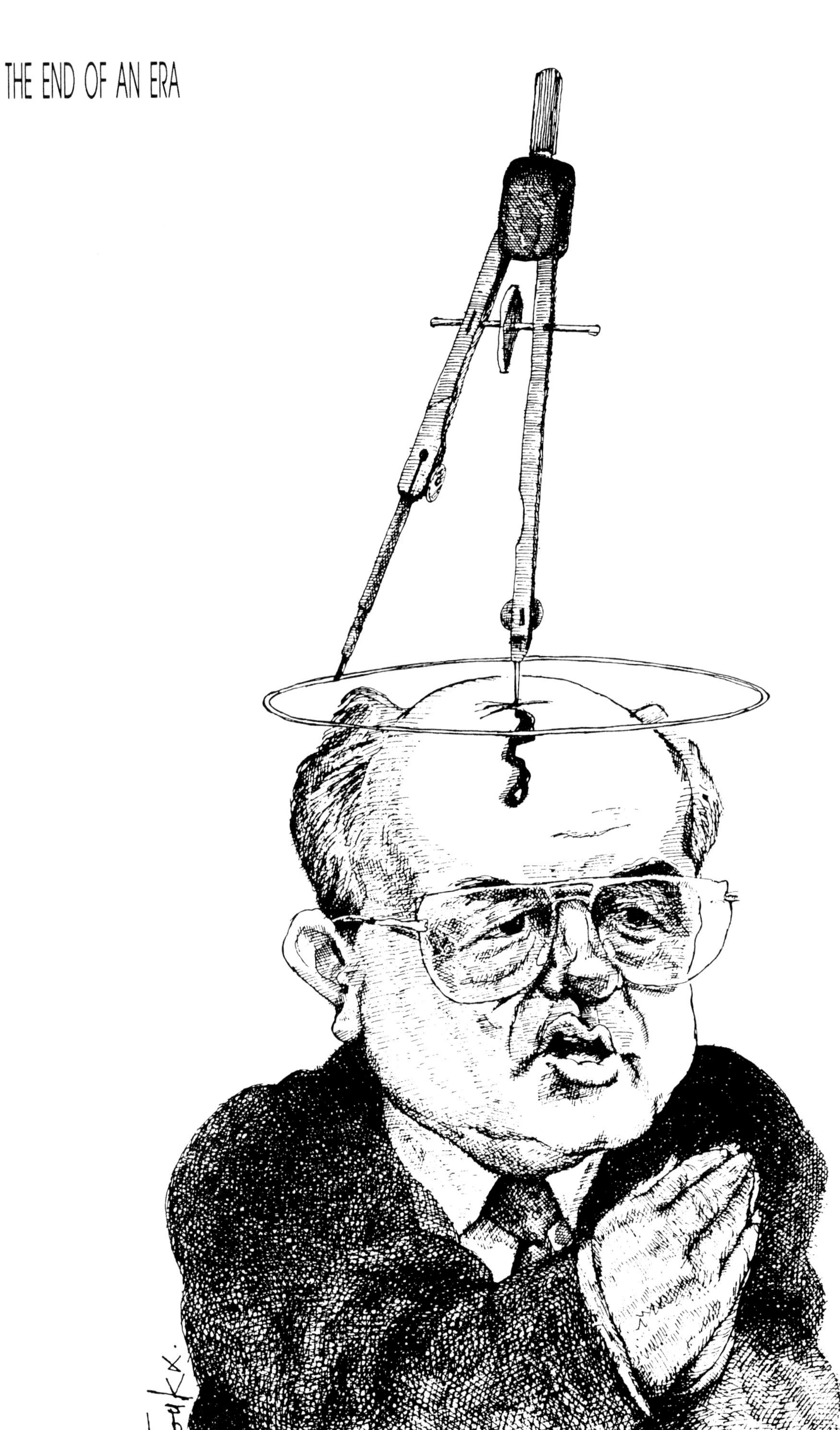

TOUKA NEYESTANI
Iran

VALERIU CURTU
Moldavia

MIKHAIL ZLATKOVSKY
Russia

ABUL MUHARRAQI
Bahrain

VALENTIN MOKIEVSKY
Estonia

GALLEGO & REY
Spain

PERESTROIKA

CARTOONISTS & WRITERS SYNDICATE

MARTYN TURNER
Ireland

TOM JANSSEN
Netherland

VALENTIN DRUZHININ
Ukraine

ATTILA BÁNÓ
Hungary

AMIR TEYMOUR AMERI
Iran

ANDRÉ PIJET
Canada

VADIM MISHUK
Russia

HABIB HADDAD
France

DAGFINN BAKKE
Norway

EDMUNDAS UNGURAITIS
Lithuania

GLASNOST...

TURHAN SELÇUK
Turkey

THE END OF AN ERA

SAULIUS MEDZIONIS
Lithuania

1961

1991

EDD ULUSCHAK
Canada

SAULIUS MEDZIONIS
Lithuania

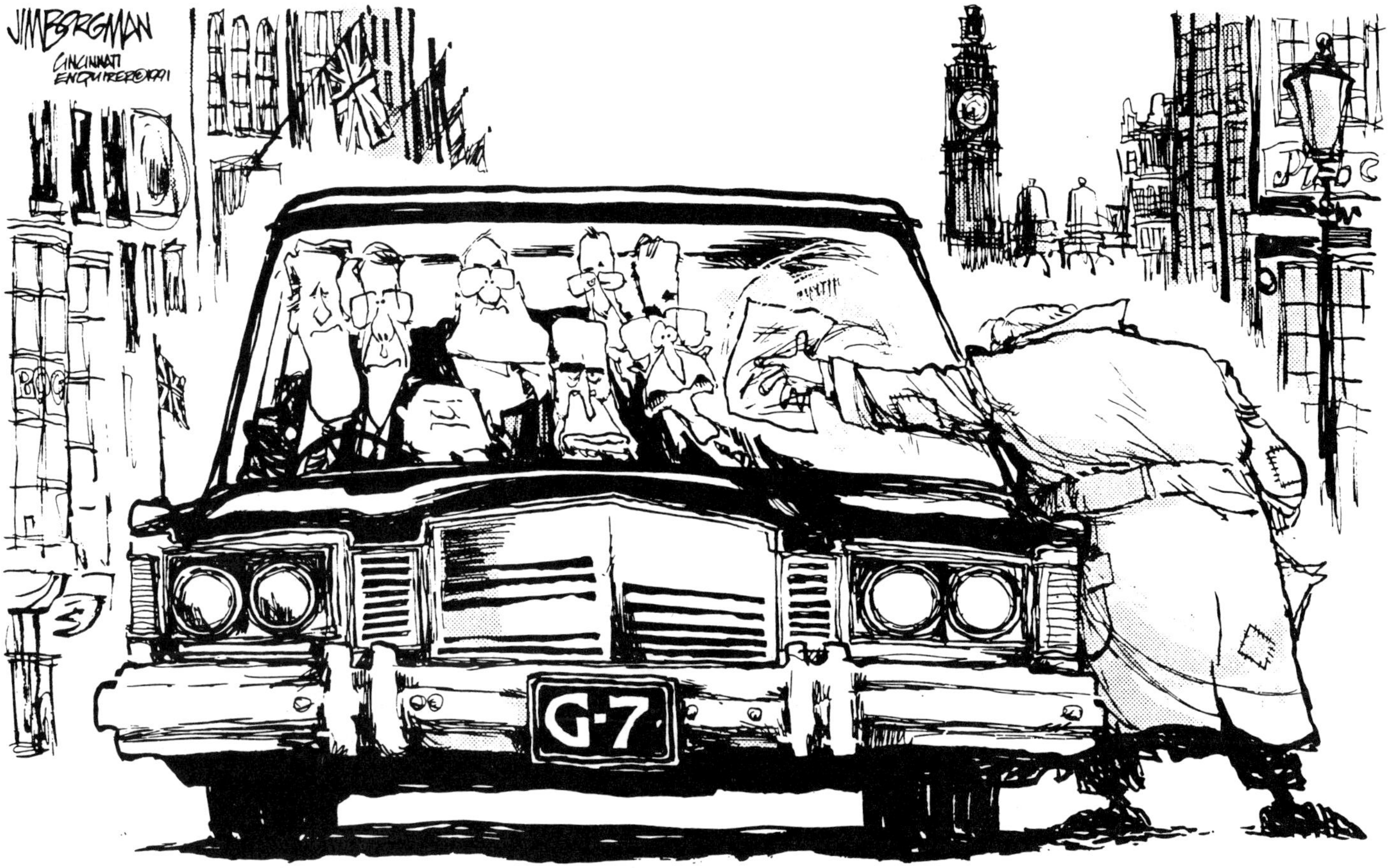

JIMBORGMAN
CINCINNATI ENQUIRER©1991
G-7

"OH PLEASE! THIS IS REALLY PATHETIC! .... COME ON, MIKHAIL, GET IN THE CAR."

JIM BORGMAN
USA

szigno

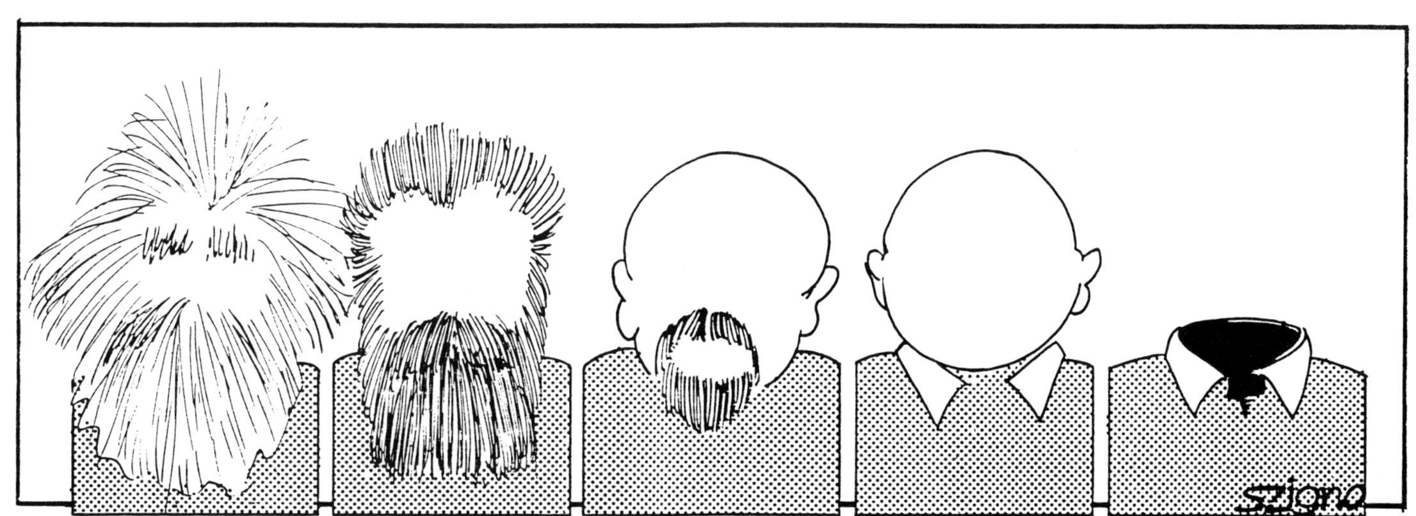

GÁBOR PÁPAI
Hungary

IGOR SMIRNOW
Russia

JÓZSEF SÁNDOR BÉKÉSI
Hungary

12·27·91 THE PHILADELPHIA INQUIRER.
UNIVERSAL PRESS SYNDICATE.

AUTH

EASTERN EUROPE

ARMS RACE

COLD WAR

SOVIET DICTATORSHIP

DEMOCRACY

I GUESS I'LL CALL IT A DAY.

TONY AUTH
USA

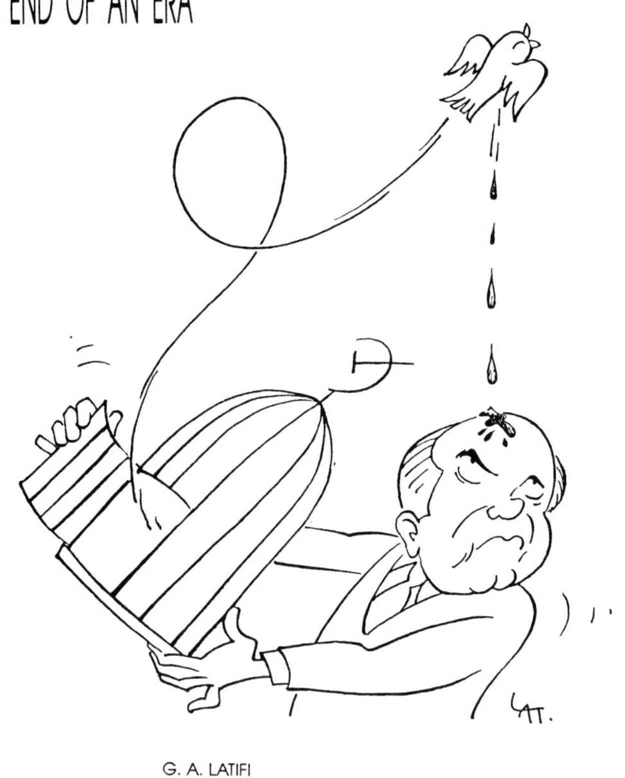

G. A. LATIFI
Iran

EDMUNDAS UNGURAITIS
Lithuania

THE BEAR FACT

I CAUGHT THERHYTHM

B. V. RAMAMURTHY
India

LÁSZLÓ GYARMATHY
Hungary

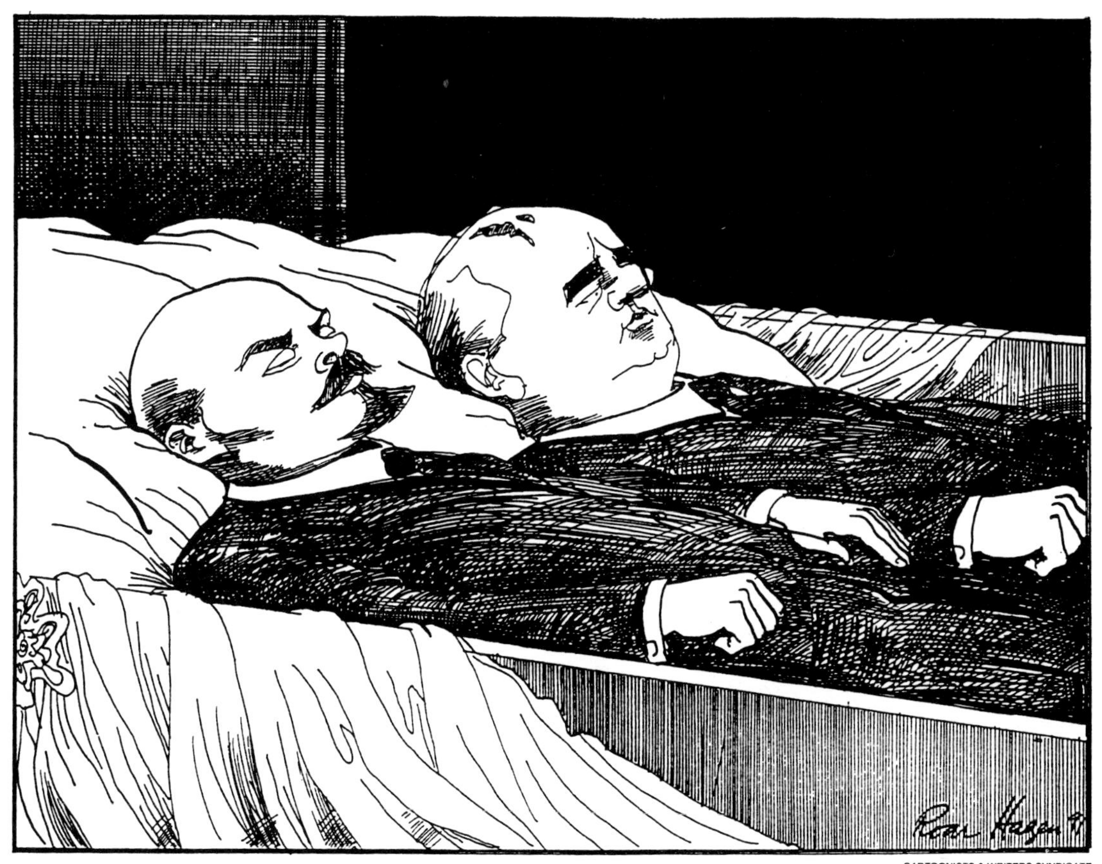

CARTOONISTS & WRITERS SYNDICATE

ROAR HAGEN
Norway

KEMCHS
Mexico

KEVIN KALLAUGHER
USA

PAUL CONRAD
USA

MOTHER RUSSIA

IGOR SMIRNOV
Russia

KEMCHS
Mexico

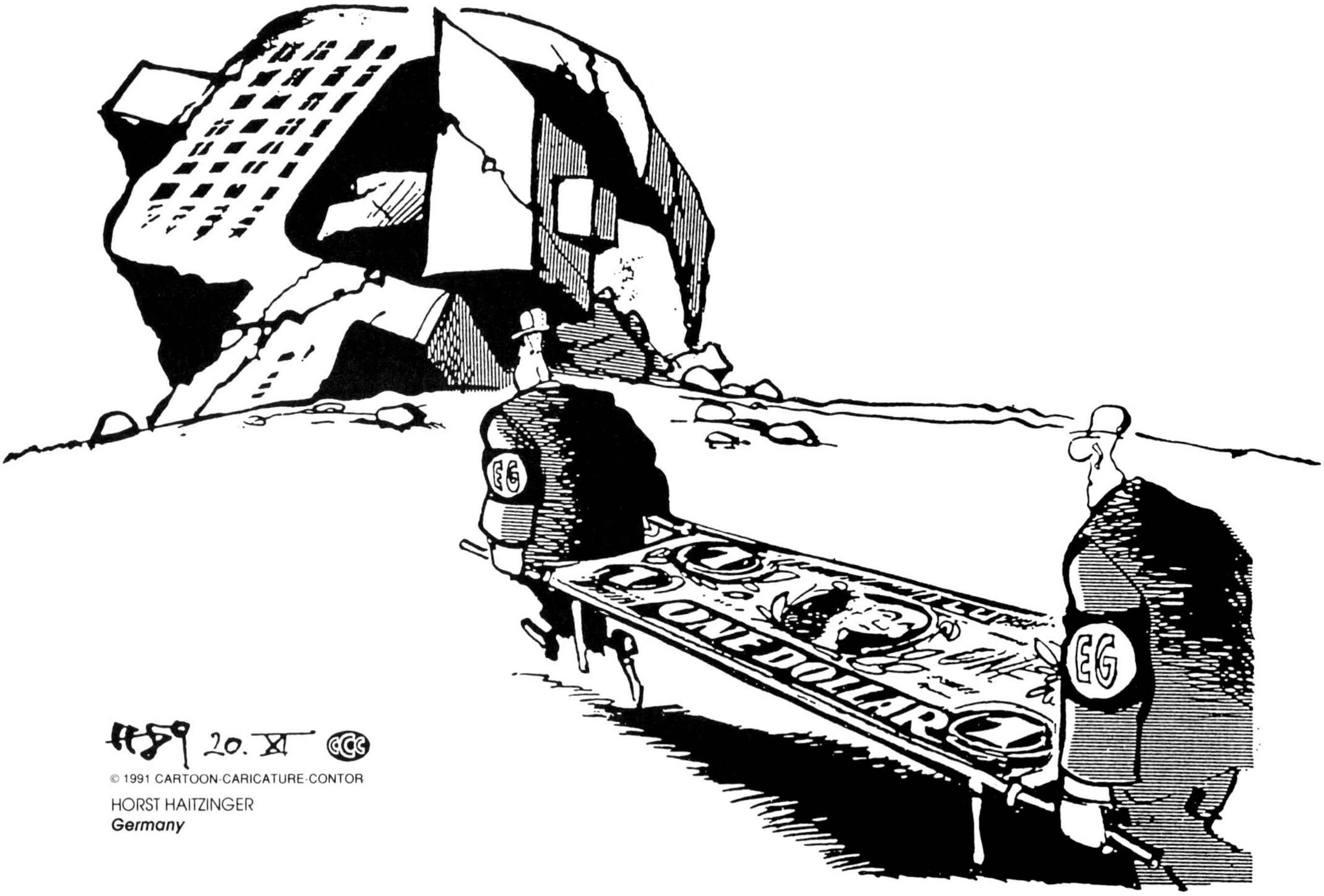

© 1991 CARTOON-CARICATURE-CONTOR

HORST HAITZINGER
Germany

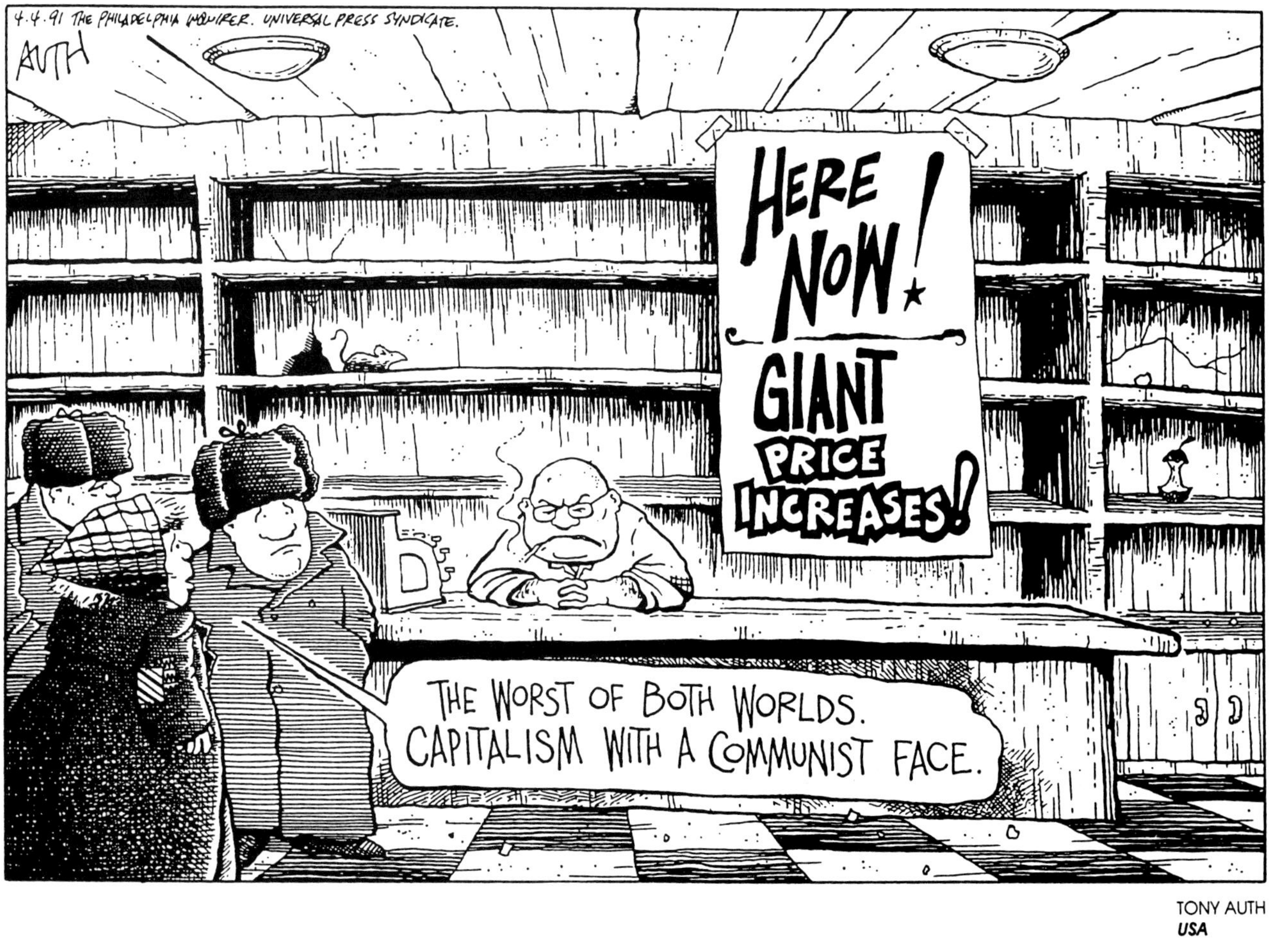

TONY AUTH
USA

KAMBIZ DERAMBAKHSH
Germany

VANCE RODEWALT
Canada

JOS COLLIGNON
Netherlands

TAN ORAL
Turkey

VALERIJ LIUBICH
Kazakhstan

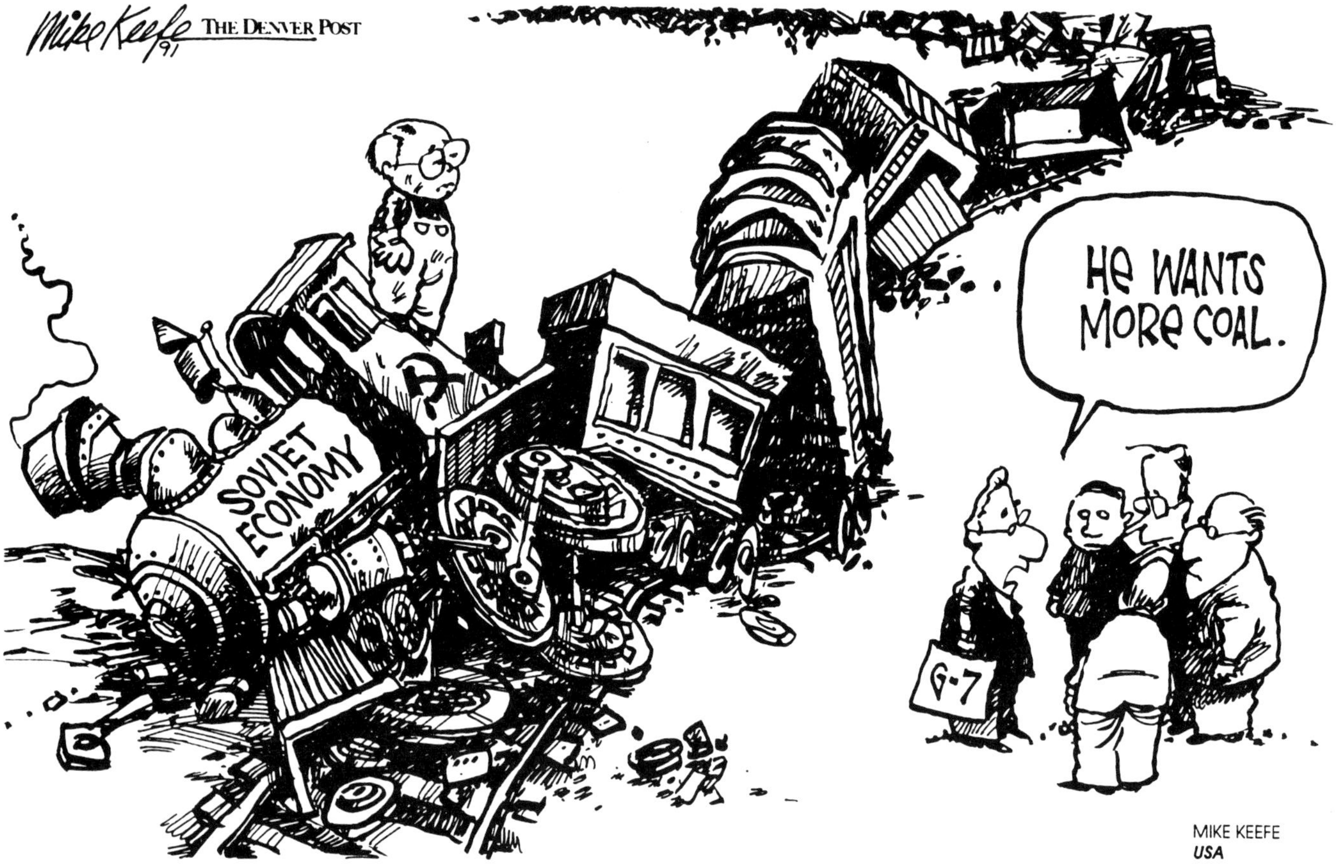
Mike Keefe 91 THE DENVER POST
SOVIET ECONOMY
HE WANTS MORE COAL.
G-7

MIKE KEEFE
USA

MARK LYNCH
Australia

IT'S A GREAT TRICK IF YOU CAN JUST KEEP THEIR MIND OFF FOOD!
MARK LYNCH.

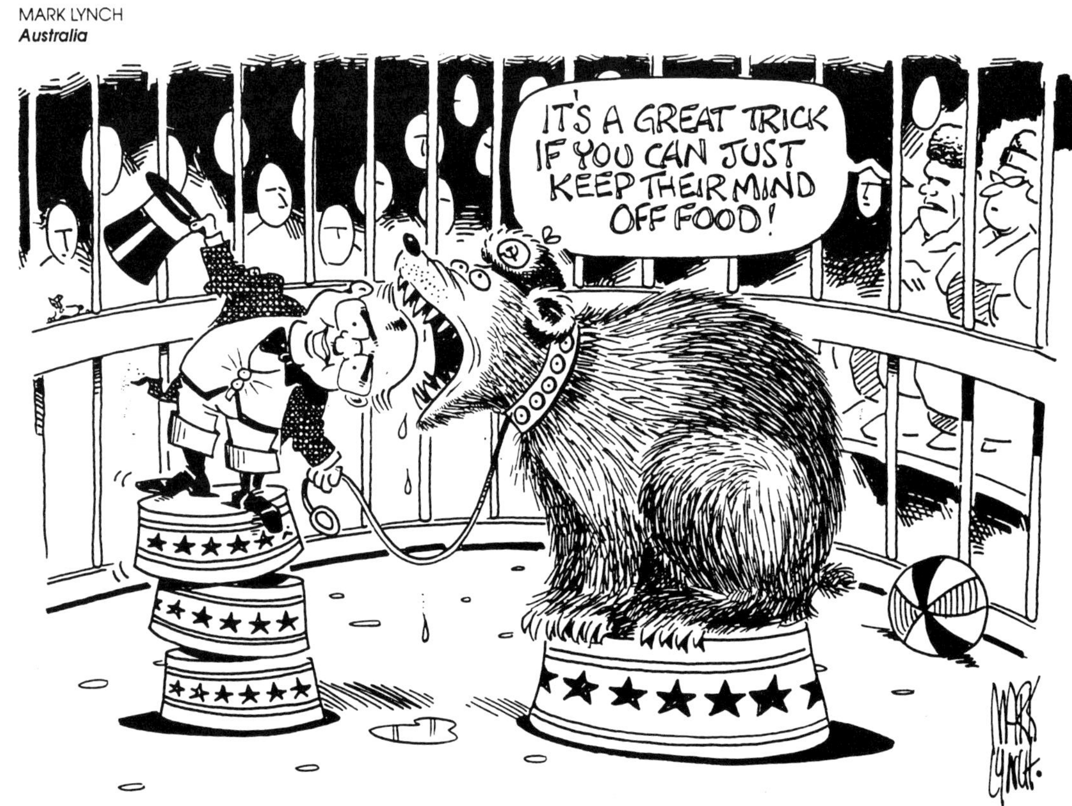

MIKHAIL ZLATKOVSKY
Russia

JIM BORGMAN
USA

R. DAMSKIS
Lithuania

A. LIEPINS
Latvia

XIN YAO ZHENG
China

SERDU
(SERGE DUHAYON)
Belgium

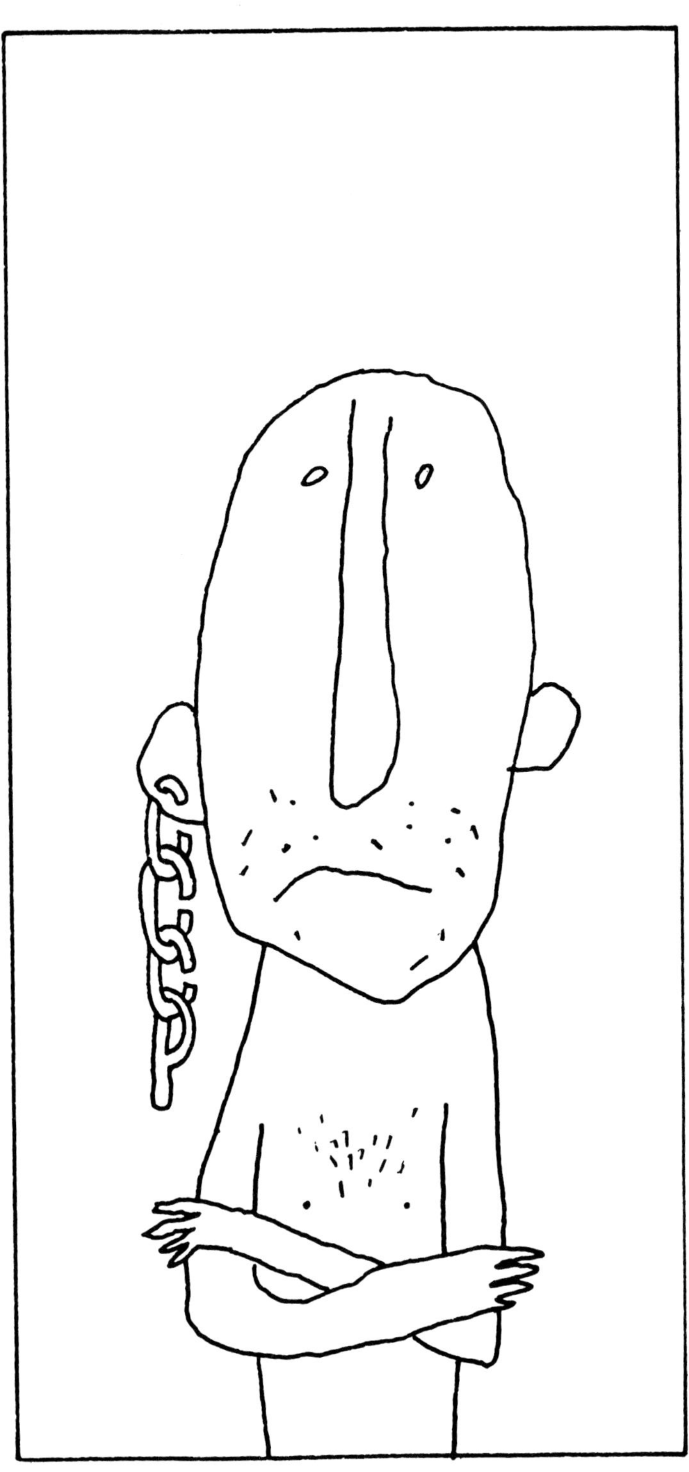

K. PODER
Estonia

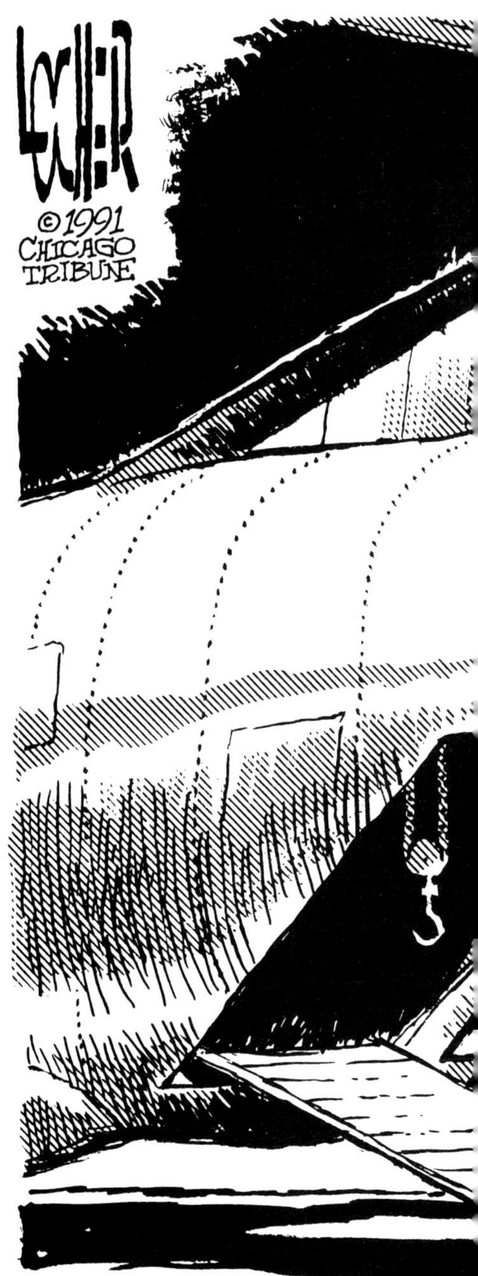

DICK LOCHER
USA

IGOR SMIRNOV
Russia

DENG COY MIEL
Philippines

GUJJAR
(B. G. GUJJARAPPA)
India

MOHAMED EFFAT ABD-EL AZIM ESMAIL
Egypt

JAVAD ALIZADEH
Iran

جواد
j a v a d.

RAGAI WANIS
Australia

MIRO STEFANOVIC
Yugoslavia

PEDRO PALMA
Portugal

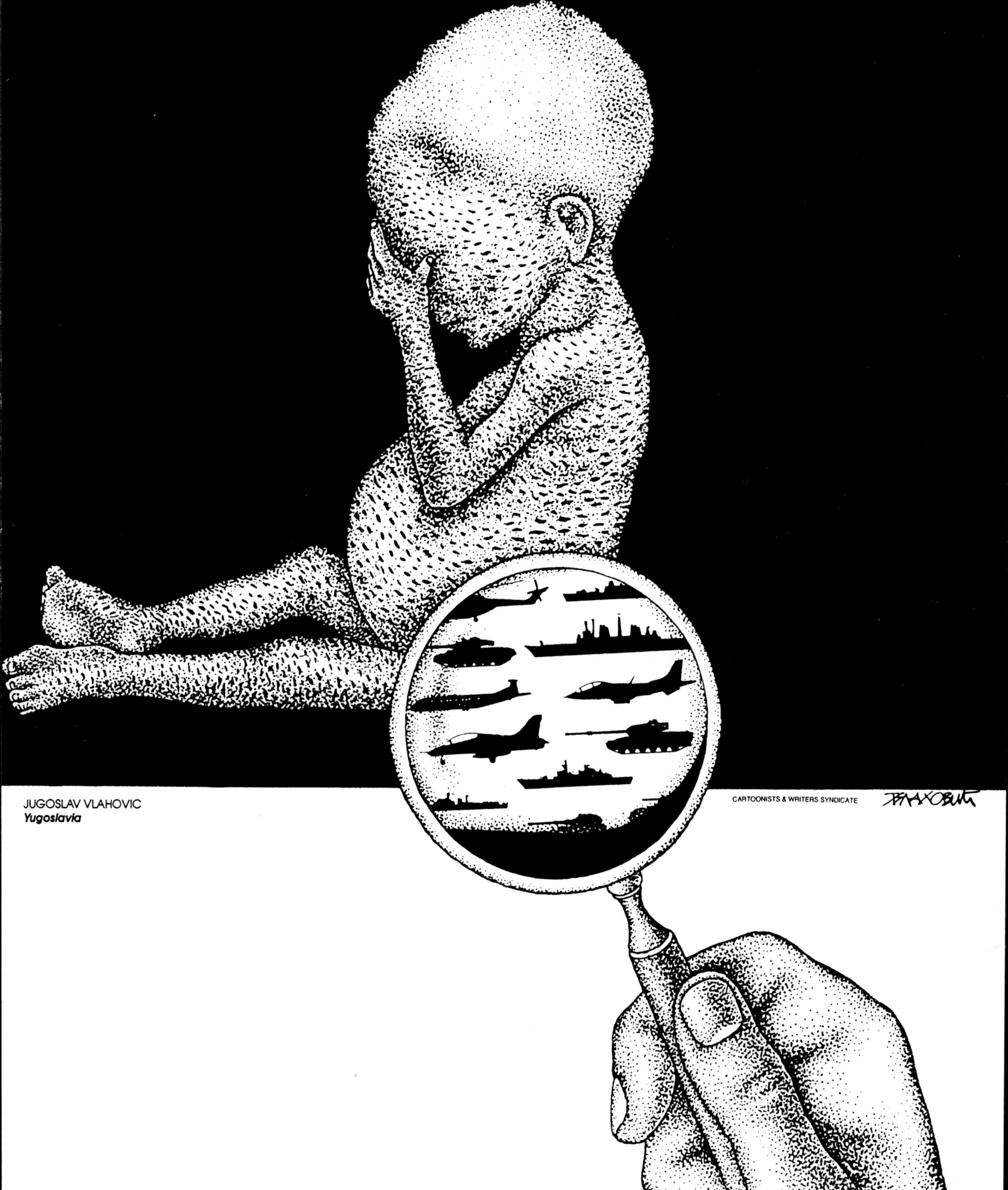
JUGOSLAV VLAHOVIC
Yugoslavia
CARTOONISTS & WRITERS SYNDICATE

JAVAD ALIZADEH
Iran

عبدالوهاب العوضي

A. A. AL-AWADI
Kuwait

DICK LOCHER
USA

IGOR SMIRNOV
Russia

JAN TOMASCHOFF
Germany

CARTOONING IN LATIN AMERICA

ENRIQUE PILOZO
Equador

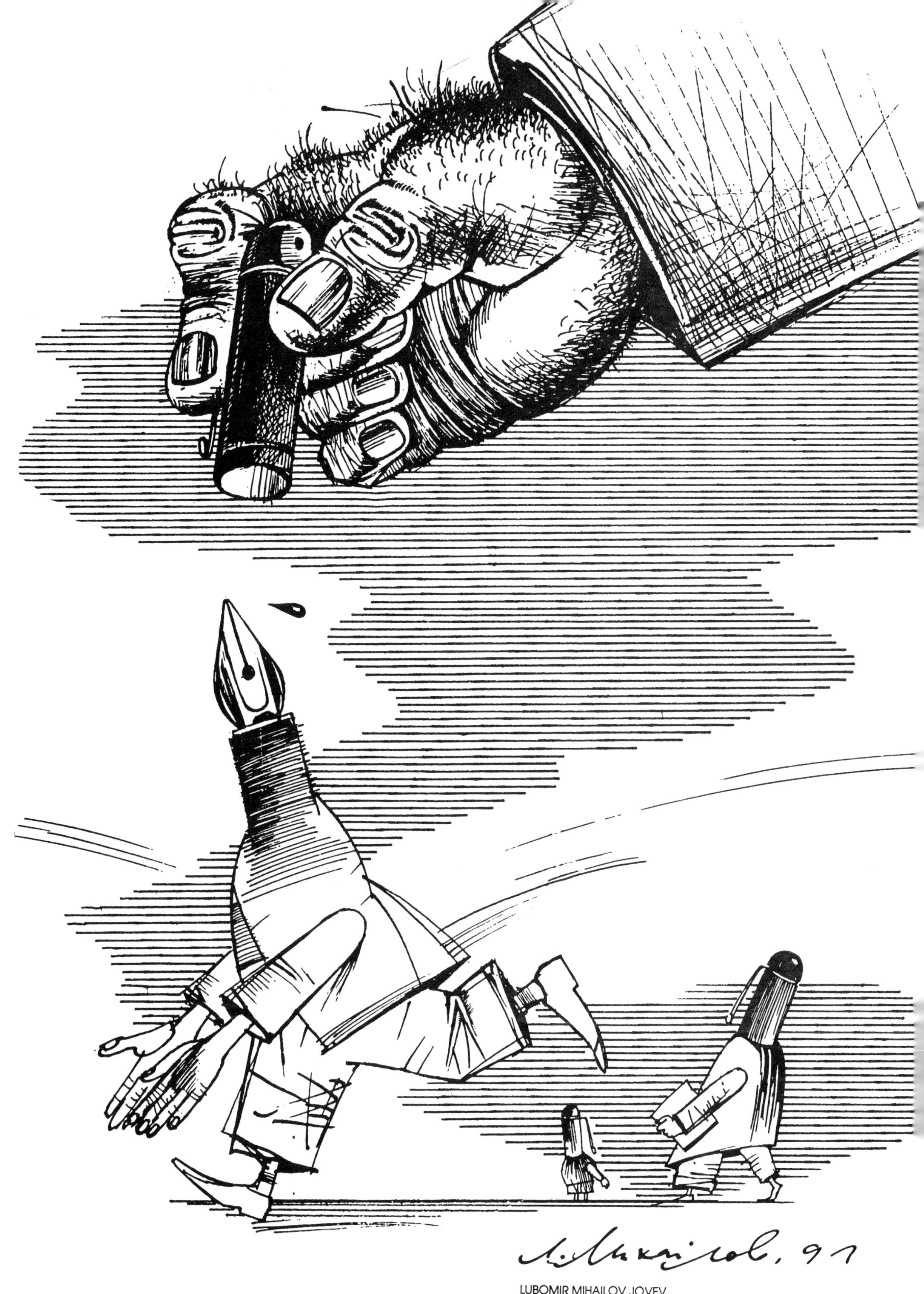

LUBOMIR MIHAILOV JOVEV
Bulgaria

DICK LOCHER
USA

SIGNE WILKINSON
USA

MARK LYNCH
Australia

DAVID ANDERSON
Canada

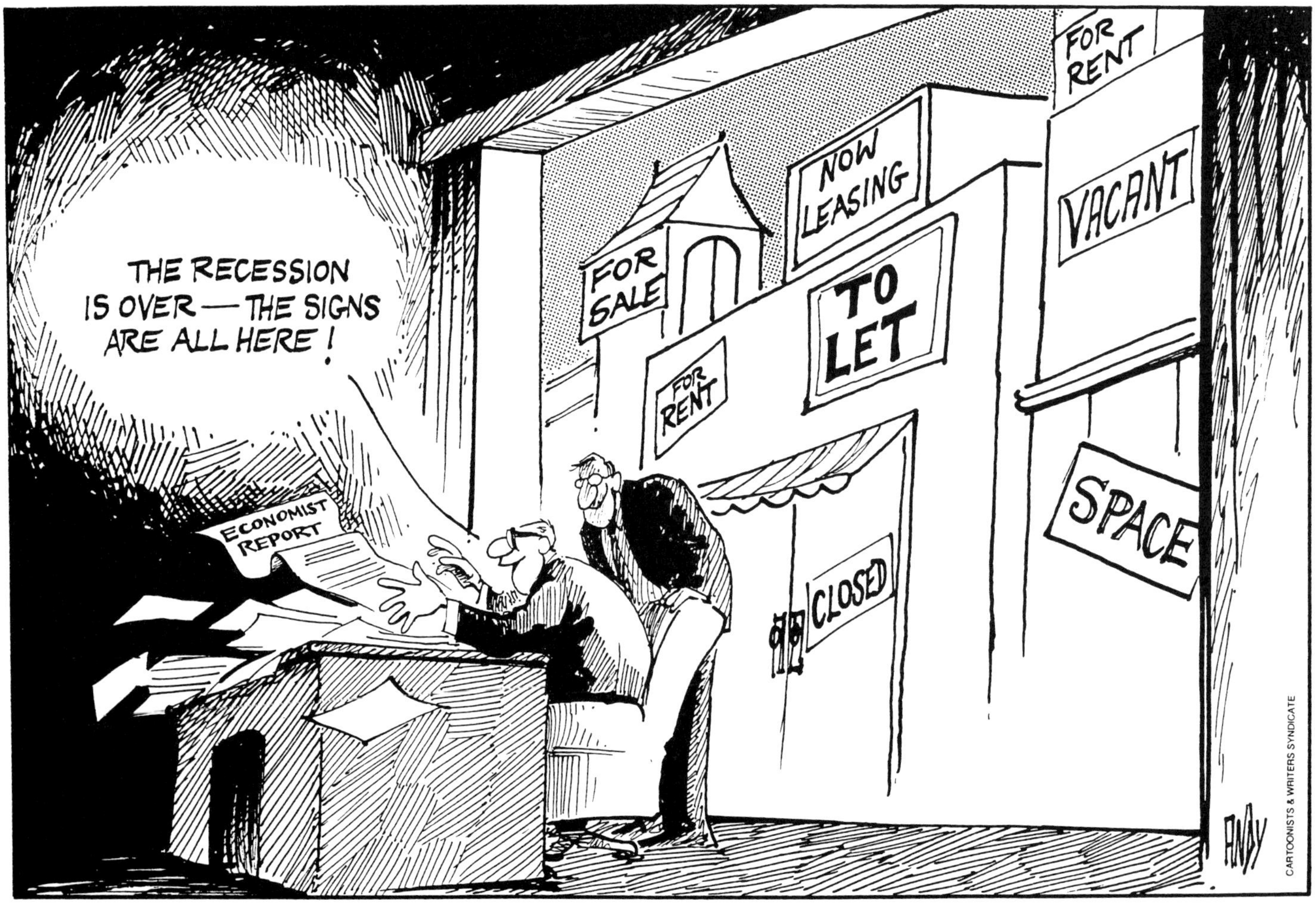

THE RECESSION IS OVER — THE SIGNS ARE ALL HERE!

ECONOMIST REPORT

FOR RENT
NOW LEASING
VACANT
FOR SALE
TO LET
FOR RENT
SPACE
CLOSED

ANDY

DENG COY MIEL
Philippines

MIKE KEEFE
USA

TANAKA MINORU
Japan

Pearl bullets are okay

JAVAD ALIZADEH
Iran

MACNELLY Chicago Tribune
PRESIDENT DOOLITTLE'S DARING RAID ON TOKYO:
Ford

JEFF MACNELLY
USA

JEFF MACNELLY
USA

ROAR HAGEN
Norway

BALTIMORE SUN · C&W SYNDICATE

KEVIN KALLAUGHER
USA

ALEKSANDER KLAS
Yugoslavia

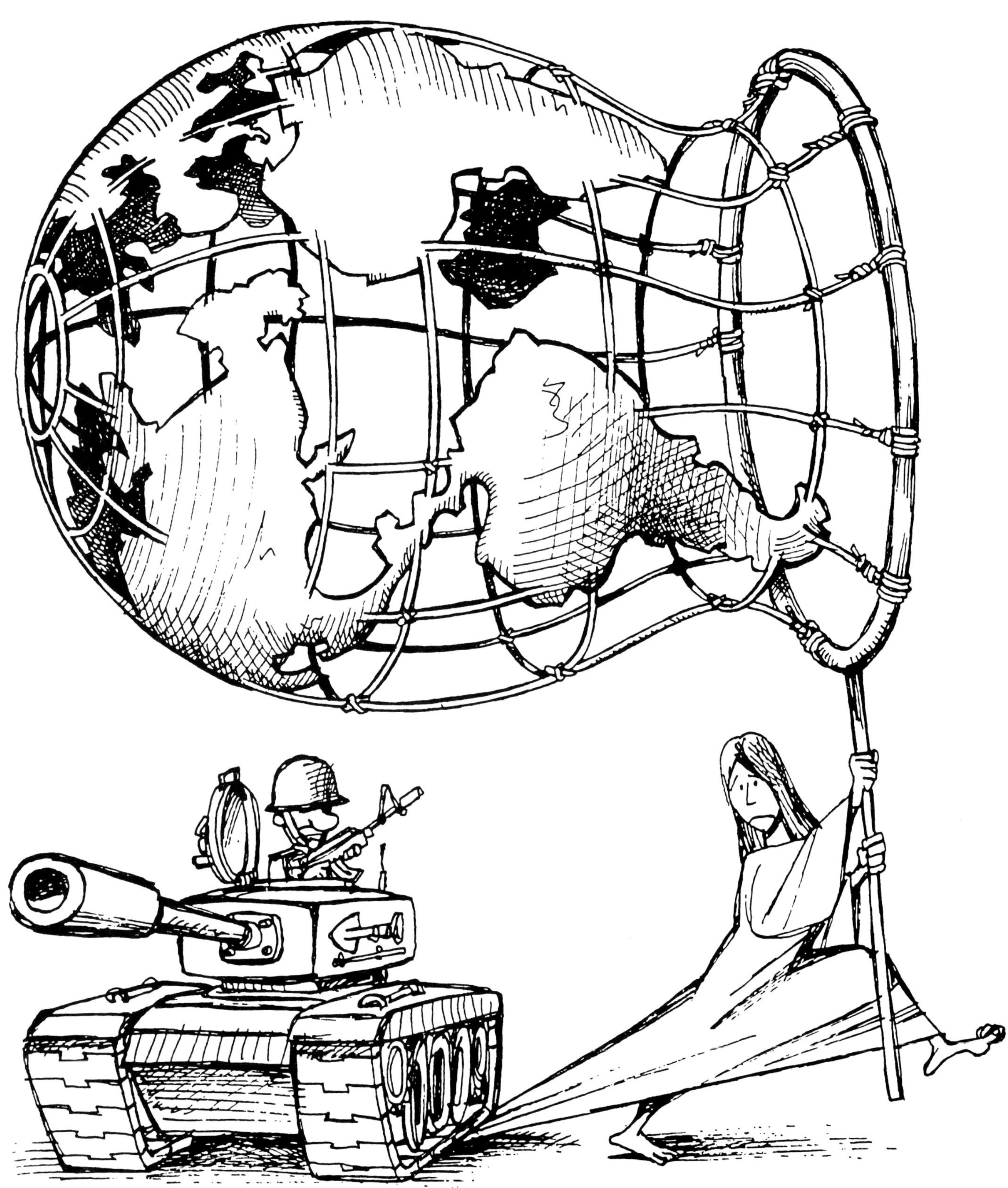

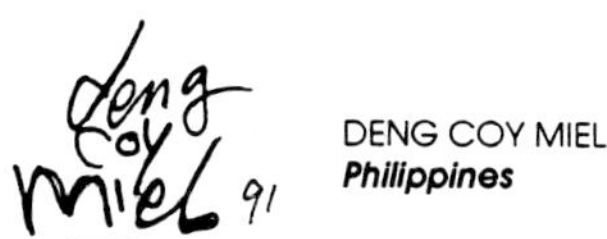

DENG COY MIEL
Philippines

AARON
Mexico

ANTÓNIO MOREIRA ANTUNES
Portugal

Mike Keefe THE DENVER POST
YUGOSLAVIA
FIRE
CEASE
FIRE
CEASE
FIRE
CEASE
FIRE
CEASE
FIRE
CEASE
FIRE
CEASE

MIKE KEEFE
USA

CHETNIK
JAN

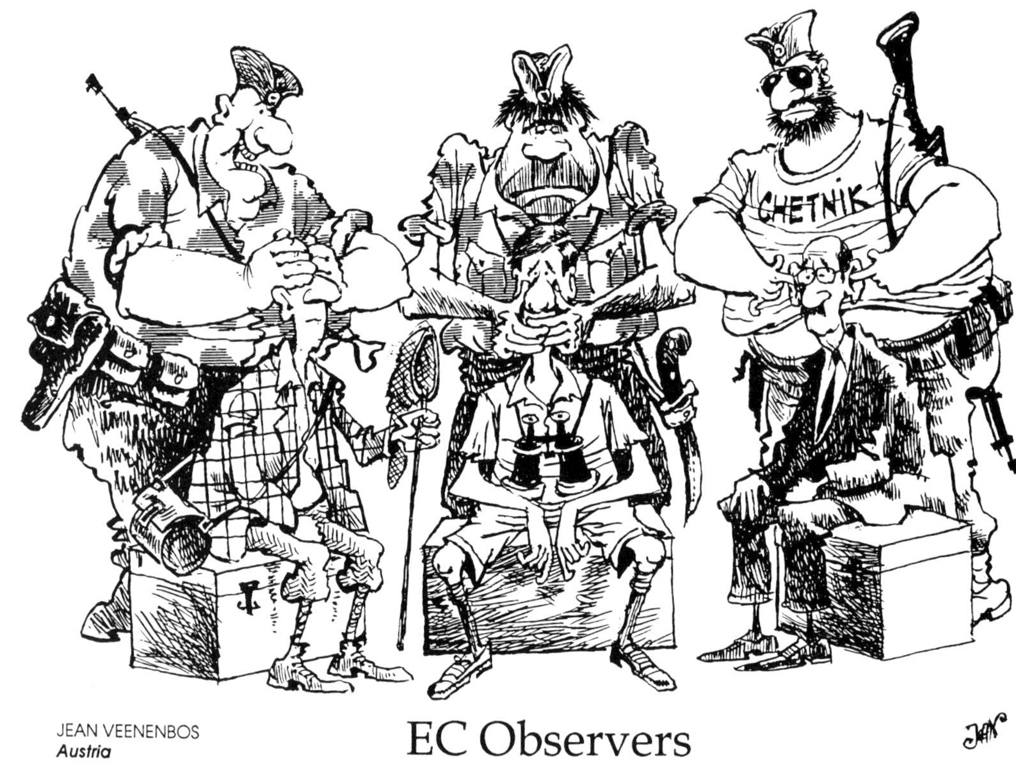

JEAN VEENENBOS
Austria

EC Observers

PETAR PISMESTROVIC
Austria

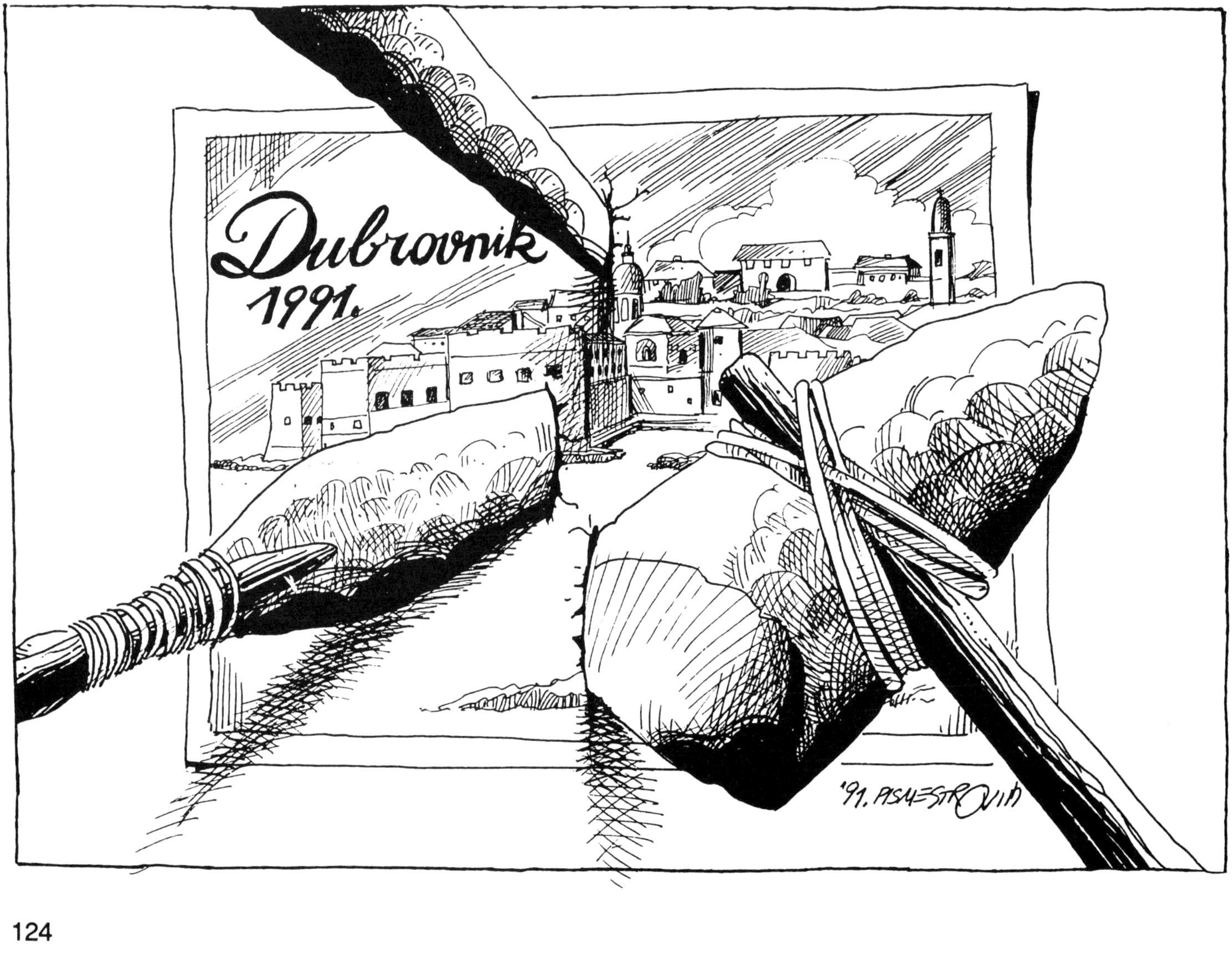
Dubrovnik
1991.
'91. PISMESTROVIĆ

JUGOSLAV VLAHOVIC
Yugoslavia

OLIVER SCHOPF
Austria

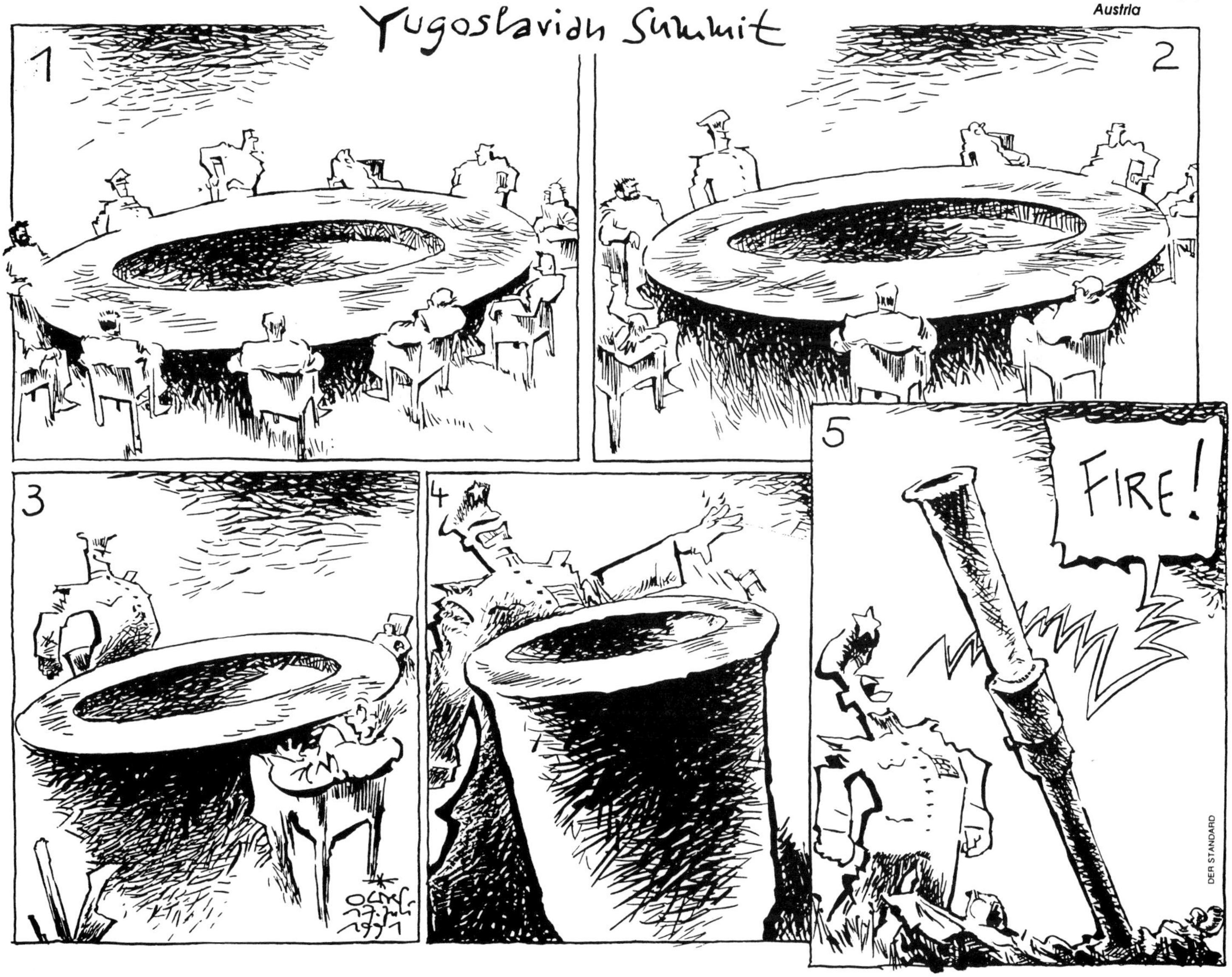

Yugoslavian Summit

1

2

3

4

5

FIRE!

DER STANDARD

CSABA JÁKÓ
Hungary

ROAR HAGEN
Norway

FELIX
(SRECKO PUNTARIC)
Croatia

HERE IS
A 13TH CENTURY MORTAR
THAT WITHSTOOD
THE BARBARIANS...

PLANTU

PLANTU
France

JIM BORGMAN
USA

ARAFAT
PLO

JANS
(JAN STJERNKVIST)
Sweden

DOMINIQUE JACQUEMIN
Belgium

HABIB HADDAD
France

MEIR RONNEN
Israel

DOMINIQUE JACQUEMIN
Belgium

DOMINIQUE JACQUEMIN
Belgium

TURHAN SELÇUK
Turkey

HABIB HADDAD
France

HELLO, YOU SCUM SUCKING MOTHER OF A BLOATED PIG

MIKE PETERS
USA

HELLO, YOU SLIME DRINKING TICK ON A CAMELS REAR.
SEE? THEY'RE TALKING.
UNITED FEATURE SYN — ©1991 DAYTON DAILY NEWS

JIM BORGMAN
USA

A FOOT IN THE DOOR

A. A. AL-AWADI
Kuwait

DOMINIQUE JACQUEMIN
Belgium

CARTOONISTS & WRITERS SYNDICATE

HENG KIM SONG
Singapore

MIK JAGO
Israel

PETAR PISMESTROVIC
Austria

STUART GOLDMAN
USA

GUJJAR
(B. G. GUJJARAPPA)
India

ZE'EV
(YA'AKOV FARKAS)
Israel

CARTOONISTS & WRITERS SYNDICATE

HARFOUSH
(EL SAIED ABD-EL KADER HAMED)
Egypt

DICK LOCHER
USA

AL AHRAM - C&W SYNDICATE
GOMAA FARHAT
Egypt

PEIN
Israel

JIM BORGMAN
USA

"PLEASE... (PUFF, PUFF!)... SIGN HERE... (PUFF! PUFF!) ...PLEASE..."

JIM BORGMAN
USA

ED STEIN
USA

G. A. LATIFI
Iran

DOUG MARLETTE
USA

KAL
(KEVIN KALLAUGHER)
USA

ARAB-ISRAELI PEACE TALKS

BAS MITROPOULOS
Greece

STEVE GREENBERG
USA

GREENBERG — SEATTLE POST-INTELLIGENCER 1991

THANK YOU FOR THAT EXAMPLE OF OPEN-MINDEDNESS, MR. AL-SHARAA. NEXT SPEAKER: MR. SHAMIR...

AARON
Mexico

DANA SUMMERS
USA

OK, WHO WANTS TO GO FIRST?
I DO! I DO!
PEACE TALKS
BAKER
THE ORLANDO SENTINEL SUMMERS 1991
PEACE TALKS
WASHINGTON POST WRITERS GROUP

DAVID ANDERSON
South Africa

PLANTU
France

JIM BERRY
USA

SHMULIK
(SHEMUEL A. KATZ)
Israel

ERETZ HAGOLAN

PAUL HOLCK
Denmark

POLITIKEN

JEFF MACNELLY
USA

DRAGAN BOSNIC
Yugoslavia

LOOK, THIS NEW WORLD ORDER SHOULD BE SEEN AS THE LAST PHASE OF A HISTORICALLY INEVITABLE DEVELOPMENT..
DON'T FORGET TO PUT A WALL AROUND IT

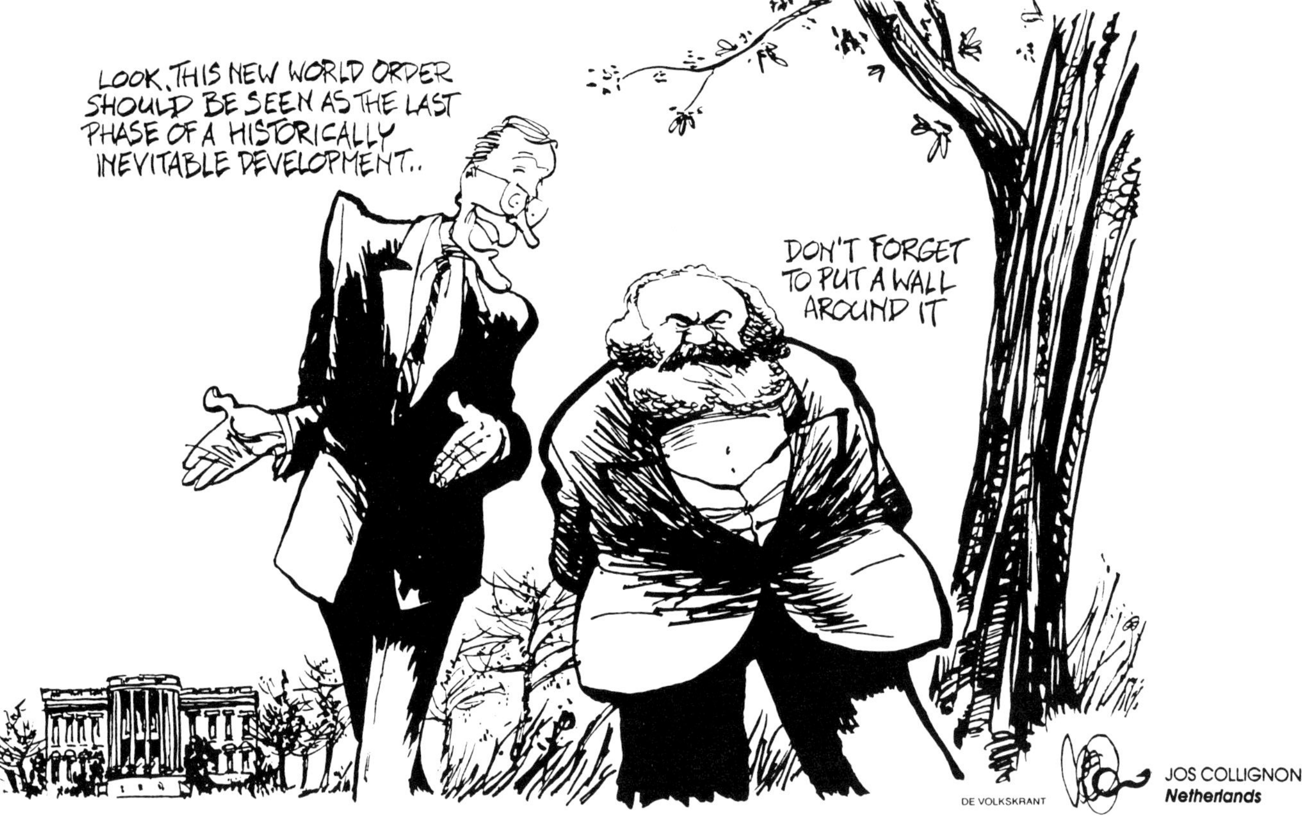

DE VOLKSKRANT

JOS COLLIGNON
Netherlands

ROY PETERSON
Canada

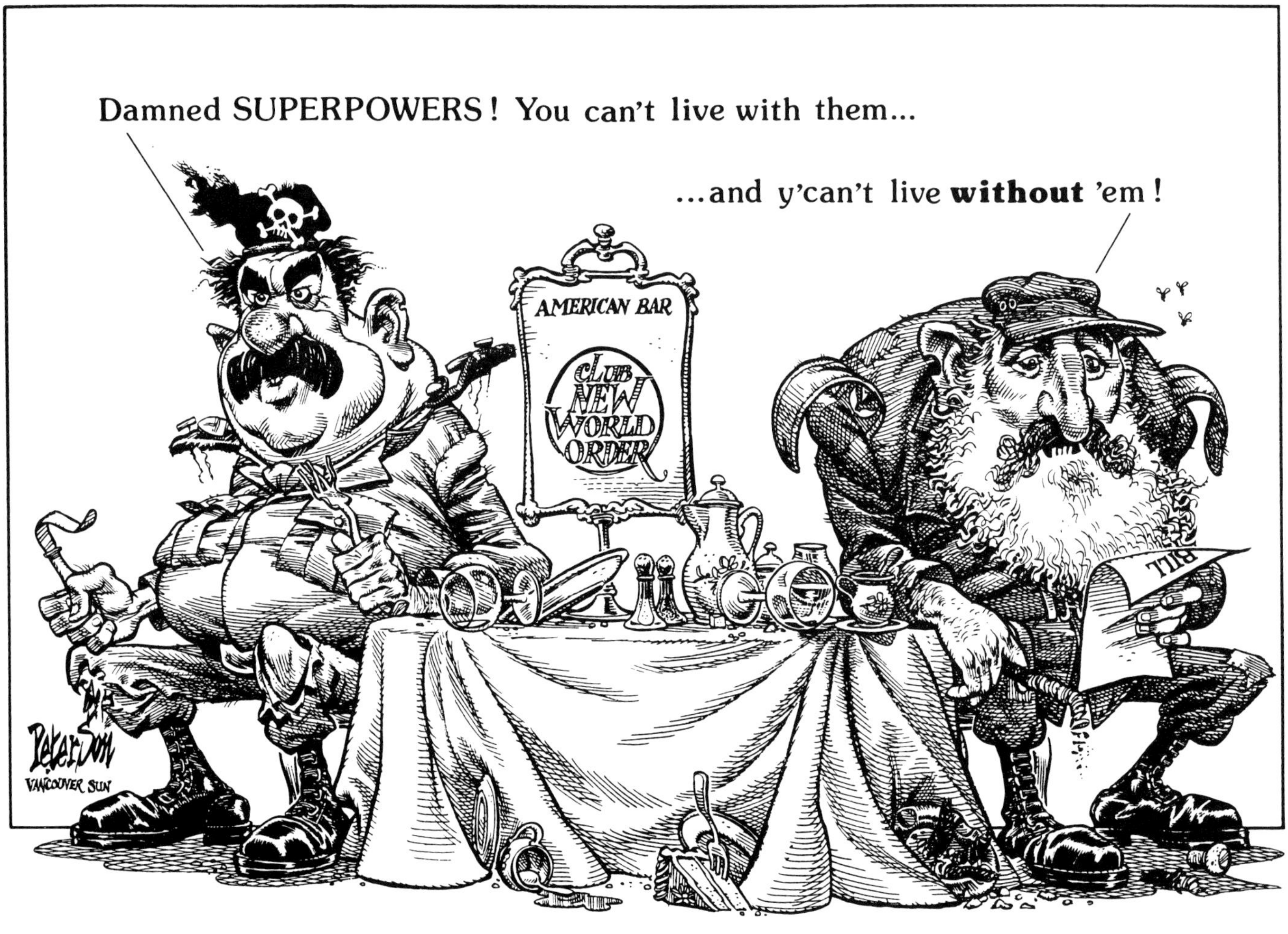
Damned SUPERPOWERS! You can't live with them...
...and y'can't live **without** 'em!
AMERICAN BAR
CLUB NEW WORLD ORDER
BILL
PETERSON
VANCOUVER SUN

THE VANCOUVER SUN, TORSTAR SYNDICATE, C&W SYNDICATE

JULES FEIFFER
USA

DOUG MARLETTE
USA

LOS ANGELES

VILNIUS

PRETORIA

WEST BANK

MARLETTE ©1991
NEW YORK NEWSDAY

TOM JANSSEN
Netherlands

ROY PETERSON
Canada

WALTER HANEL
Germany

SERDU
(SERGE DUHAYON)
Belgium

Index

Argentina
ROBERTO FONTANARROSA 55

Australia
MARK LYNCH 8, 36, 86, 108
RAGAI WANIS 96

Austria
PETAR PISMESTROVIC 6, 124, 141
OLIVER SCHOPF 125
JEAN VEENENBOS 124

Bahrain
ABUL MUHARRAQI

Belgium
DOMINIQUE JACQUEMIN
50, 131, 133, 134, 139
SERDU (SERGE DUHAYON)
51, 89, 163

Bulgaria
FIKO FIKOV 35
LUBOMIR MIHAILOV JOVEV 105

Canada
DAVID ANDERSON 46, 108, 152
JOSH BEUTEL 29
ROY PETERSON 41, 52, 57, 156, 161
ANDRÉ PIJET 68
VANCE RODEWALT 41, 83
JAMES TODD 23
EDD ULUSCHAK 72

China
ZHANG, YAONING 20
ZHENG, XIN YAO 89

Croatia
FELIX (SRECKO PUNTARIC) 127

Czechoslovakia
VLADIMIR BALCAR 33, 60

Denmark
PAUL HOLCK 153
PREBEN OLESEN 47

Egypt
MOHAMED EFFAT ABD-EL AZIM
ESMAIL 95
GOMAA FARHAT 144
HARFOUSH
(EL SAIED ABD-EL KADER HAMED) 143
ALADIN SAAD 10

England
CHARLES GRIFFIN 9, 42, 42,

Ecuador
FRANCISCO CAJAS 22
ENRIQUE PILOZO 104

Estonia
VALENTIN MOKIEVSKY 65
K. PODER 90

France
HABIB HADDAD 69, 132, 136
PANCHO (FRANCISCO GRAELLS) 8, 61
PLANTU 127, 152

Germany
KAMBIZ DERAMBAKHSH 46, 83
KARL GERD 43
RAINER HACHFELD 45
HORST HAITZINGER 24, 82
WALTER HANEL 162
BARBARA HENNIGER 43
JAN TOMASCHOFF 44, 104

Greece
BAS MITROPOULOS 57, 150

Honduras
NAPOLEON HAM 48

Hungary
ATTILA BÁNÓ 68
JÓZSEF SÁNDOR BÉKÉSI 20, 75
LÁSZLÓ GYARMATHY 77
CSABA JÁKÓ 126
GÁBOR PÁPAI 73

India
GUJJAR (B. G. GUJJARAPPA)
39, 94, 142
B. V. RAMAMURTHY 76
PRABHAKAR WAIRKAR 49

Iran
JAVAD ALIZADEH
25, 96, 100, 111
AMIR TEYMOUR AMERI 68
G. A. LATIFI 13, 76, 147
TOUKA NEYESTANI 62

Ireland
MARTYN TURNER 32, 66

Israel
MIK JAGO 140
PEIN 145
MEIR RONNEN 132
SHMULIK (SHEMUEL A. KATZ) 13, 153
ZE'EV (YA'AKOV FARKAS) 143

Italy
ALDO BARTOLOTTI 24
MARCO DE ANGELIS 54

Japan
TANAKA MINORU 110

Kazakhstan
VALERIJ LIUBICH 85

Kuwait
A. A. AL-AWADI 101

Latvia
A. LIEPINS 88

Lithuania
R. DAMSKIS 88
SAULIUS MEDZIONIS 72, 72
EDMUNDAS UNGURAITIS 70, 76

Mexico
AARON 120, 151
KEMCHS 78, 81

Moldavia
VALERIU CURTU 63

Netherlands
FRITZ BEHRENDT 54
JOS COLLIGNON 7, 84, 156
TOM JANSSEN 66, 160

Norway
DAGFINN BAKKE 70
ROAR HAGEN 28, 77, 115, 126

Peru
MARCO RAMOS TRUJILLANO 20

Philippines
DENG COY MIEL 93, 109, 118

Poland
ANTONI CHODOROWSKI 37
SZYMON KOBYLINSKI 36

Portugal
ANTÓNIO MOREIRA ANTUNES
4, 59, 121
PEDRO PALMA 9, 98

Romania
PAVEL BOTEZATU 56

Russia
VADIM MISHUK 68
IGOR SMIRNOW 74, 80, 92, 103
MIKHAIL ZLATKOVSKY 64, 87

Singapore
HENG KIM SONG 140

South Africa
JOCK LAYDEN 21
TONY GROGAN 21

Spain
GALLEGO & REY 65

Sweden
JANS (JAN STJERNKVIST) 130
GUSTAVE EWERT KARLSSON 36

Turkey
TAN ORAL 85
TURHAN SELÇUK 71, 135
ALPER SUSUZLU 58

Ukraine
VALENTIN DRUZHININ 67

United States of America
TONY AUTH 11, 18, 26, 75, 82
JIM BERRY 153
JIM BORGMAN 14, 34, 73,
88, 128, 138, 145, 146
PAUL CONRAD 12, 15, 79
JEFF DANZIGER 19, 47
JULES FEIFFER 6, 157
STUART GOLDMAN 142
STEVE GREENBERG 150
KAL (KEVIN KALLAUGHER)
45, 78, 116, 149
MIKE KEEFE 49, 86, 110, 122
DICK LOCHER 91, 102, 106, 144
JEFF MACNELLY
31, 38, 113, 114, 154
DOUG MARLETTE 40, 148, 158
PAT OLIPHANT 14, 16, 35, 61
MIKE PETERS 137
DAVID SEAVEY 23, 30
ED STEIN 34, 146
DANA SUMMERS 22, 51, 151
PAUL SZÉP 29
SIGNE WILKINSON 107

Yugoslavia
DRAGAN BOSNIC 155
ALEKSANDER KLAS 117
MIRO STEFANOVIC 97
JUGOSLAV VLAHOVIC 99, 125

MORCHOISNE / MULATIER / RICORD ★ *France* © GRAPHIC GRINS

DENG COY MIEL ★ *Philippines*